Softshell Turtle

Softshell Turtle Pet Owner's Guide.

Softshell Turtle Care, Behavior, Diet, Interacting, Costs and Health.

By

Ben Team

ALL RIGHTS RESERVED. This book contains material protected under International and Federal Copyright Laws and Treaties.

Any unauthorized reprint or use of this material is strictly prohibited. No part of this book may be reproduced or transmitted in any form or by any means, electronic, mechanical or otherwise, including photocopying or recording, or by any information storage and retrieval system without express written permission from the author.

Copyrighted © 2017

Published by: IMB Publishing

Table of Contents

Table of Contents 3

About The Author 5

Foreword 5

PART I: THE SOFTSHELL TURTLE 7

Chapter 1: Softshell Turtle Description and Anatomy 8

Chapter 2: Softshell Turtle Biology and Behavior 14

Chapter 3: Classification and Taxonomy 17

Chapter 4: The Softshell Turtle's World 20

PART II: SOFTSHELL TURTLE HUSBANDRY 22

Chapter 5: Softshell Turtles as Pets 23

Chapter 6: Providing the Captive Habitat 30

Chapter 7: Water Quality and Filtration 35

Chapter 8: Heating and Lighting 37

Chapter 9: Substrate and Furniture 46

Chapter 10: Maintaining the Captive Habitat 50

Chapter 11: Feeding Softshell Turtles 56

Chapter 12: Interacting with Your Softshell Turtle 59

Chapter 13: Common Health Concerns 61

Chapter 14: Breeding Softshell Turtles 67

Chapter 15: Further Reading 77

References 82

Index **83**

About The Author

The author, Ben Team, is an environmental educator and author with over 16 years of professional reptile-keeping experience. Ben currently maintains www.FootstepsInTheForest.com, where he shares information, narration and observations of the natural world. When not writing about plants, animals and habitats, Ben enjoys spending time with his beautiful wife.

Foreword

Much of the appeal of pet reptiles arises from their otherwordly nature.

Unlike dogs and cats, who are familiar, close relatives of humans, reptiles emerged from a more basal branch of the family tree.

Instead of hair, they're covered in scaley skin. Instead of a high-octane metabolism, their bodies routinely slow down to save energy. Instead of the gregarious nature of many mammals, they typically prefer to live alone.

And there body plans are equally unique; from snakes who lack legs, to crocodilians who bear armor-plated skin and huge jaws, most reptiles are built completely differently than mammals are.

But among reptiles, none are more unique than turtles. Turtles are clad in scaly skin, as most other reptiles, and most have ectothermic metabolisms like other reptiles, but each one is covered by a large, protective shell.

Currently, scientists recognize 346 turtle species worldwide, but only a small handful of these are appropriate and available for reptile keepers. Many grow too large, or require far too much space to make suitable captives, while others are too rare to be suitable for collection for the pet trade.

This leaves perhaps two or three dozen species that make suitable choices for pets. Many are quite similar to each other, if not the other animals of the world. For example, Russian tortoises (*Testudo horsefieldii*) and leopard tortoises (*Stigmochelys pardalis*) are built in relatively similar ways, and the biggest difference between them come down to size. The same could be said of painted turtles (*Chrysemys picta*) and red eared sliders (*Trachemys scripta scripta*).

But a few turtle lineages are quite different from most others. The seven living sea turtle species, for example, have flippers rather than feet, and many feature extraordinary adaptations for their marine lifestyles.

But while sea turtles are completely unsuitable for private ownership, there are other unique turtles that make interesting and unusual captives: the softshelled turtles (Family Trionychidae).

***

Classified in some 15 genera and dozens of individual species, softshell turtles exhibit plenty of inter-familial diversity. However, they all share a rather similar body plan and broadly similar lifestyle.

Unlike the hard, keratin-covered shells of most turtles, softshell turtles have leathery, skin-covered shells that often exhibit some degree of flexibility near the margin. They are still comprised of bone internally, just as the shells of other turtles are, but they are different in many other ways.

These unusual shells alter the ways in which softshell turtles defend themselves and live. Many spend their time buried under the sand at the bottom of rivers, with only their heads sticking up. Most are also quite fast, as their streamlined shells help them to fly through the water, in pursuit of fish and other edible species.

Because only a handful of softshell turtles are appropriate and available for hobbyists, we'll largely focus on the softshell turtles of the genus *Apalone*, which contains those species most commonly seen in captivity.

PART I: THE SOFTSHELL TURTLE

Properly caring for any animal requires an understanding of the species and its place in the natural world. This includes digesting subjects as disparate as anatomy and ecology, diet and geography, and reproduction and physiology.

It is only by learning what your pet is, how it lives, what it does that you can achieve the primary goal of animal husbandry: Providing your pet with the highest quality of life possible.

Chapter 1: Softshell Turtle Description and Anatomy

Softshell turtles (Family Trionychidae) have a very different morphology than most other aquatic chelonians, and they exhibit a number of characteristics that are unique to the group.

The most striking difference is certainly their soft, leathery shell, which differs markedly from the hard shells of most other turtles.

Yet despite the unique morphology of softshell turtles, they possess a typical, bilaterally symmetric vertebrate body plan, including a head, long neck, tail, and four legs.

Size

Softshell turtles are medium to large turtles. Hatchlings of the genus *Apalone* – the most commonly kept species -- measure about 1 1/2 inches (4 centimeters) long and weigh about one-fifth of an ounce (5 grams) when they emerge from their eggs.

Adult softshell turtles are medium to large turtles, and most species are strongly sexually dimorphic. This means that the sexes reach different sizes. Specifically, the females grow much larger than the males do.

Mature males of the genus *Apalone*, for example, typically measure between 6 and 12 inches (15 to 30 centimeters) in straight-line shell length, while females generally measure between 12 and 24 inches (30 to 60 centimeters).

However, while a 24-inch-long turtle is indeed a large animal, many grow to more than twice this size. For example, Cantor's giant softshell (*Pelochelys cantorii*) – may reach nearly 6 feet (180 centimeters) in length.

Color and Pattern

Most softshell turtles are drably colored.

Dorsally, they typically feature an earth-toned ground color, somewhere between dark green and brown – many are olive-colored. Most have a variety of darker markings scattered over their bodies, which can take the form of dots, dashes and hollow circles. However, many older specimens, become essentially patternless with time.

Ventrally, softshell turtles are usually light green, yellowish or nearly white. Dark markings may or may not be present on the plastron.

Shell

Turtles are firmly attached to their shells; they cannot crawl out of them, as is frequently seen in cartoons and comic strips. Accordingly, a turtle's shell grows along with the turtle and remains a permanent fixture throughout its entire life.

As referenced earlier, softshell turtles have very unusual shells, relative to those of other turtles. Unlike the shells of most species, which are created from a combination of rib bones, dermal plates (bony plates that originate within the skin) and keratinized plates, called scutes, which cover the entire shell; softshell turtles lack keratinized plates and have a sharply reduced number of dermal plates. Instead of plates, their shells are covered by thick, leathery skin.

Rib bones are still intertwined with the shell, which provides the rigidity found at the center of the shell. However, there are many gaps in these bones along the margin of the shell, making the margin much more flexible than those of many other turtle species.

The top portion of a turtle's shell is called the carapace, while the bottom portion is called the plastron.

The Softshell Turtle Head

The heads of softshell turtles are somewhat small, and highly modified to suit their lifestyle. The overall design is very streamlined to help reduce water resistance. Softshell turtles have two eyes, which are normally light in color, and a snorkel- or pig-like nose that helps them breathe while remaining underwater.

Like all other living turtles, softshells lack teeth. Instead, they have a bony beak-like mouth. However, unlike most other turtle species, who have a sharp, keratin-covered beak that features a cutting surface; softshell turtles have fleshy, rubbery "lips" that cover the beak.

However, this is a case in which looks can be very deceiving. While the lips may not appear very intimidating, they cover a hard-edged bone, which is strong enough to crack open mollusk shells.

The unique heads of softshell turtles are connected to their bodies via very long necks, which allow them to raise their heads above the surface of the water while sitting on the bottom. These long necks also enable the turtles to better defend themselves, as their powerful mouths are able to reach carelessly placed fingers trying to pick them up.

Limbs and Feet

Softshell turtles have three-clawed feet (hence their familial name: Trionychidae – meaning three claws). They are extensively webbed to better help the turtles swim through the water.

Their limbs are quite powerful, enabling softshell turtles to not only swim quickly, but also scoot across dry ground much faster than other turtle species can.

Many softshell species exhibit sexual dimorphism with respect to their claws. Males have longer claws on the front limbs, which presumably play a role in the mating process; while females have longer claws on the back limbs, which presumably helps them to excavate egg chambers.

Tail

Softshell turtles have fairly unremarkable tails, although they do exhibit a strong degree of sexual dimorphism. Males have long, thick, muscular tails, while the tails of most females are much shorter and thinner. The vent of males is located beyond the margin of the shell, while those of females are located near the margin.

Internal Anatomy

While the average turtle keeper need not understand the internal anatomy of their pet enough to perform exploratory surgery, a basic understanding of the turtle's internal world is helpful.

In most respects, softshell turtles have internal anatomy that is similar to that of other vertebrates, such as humans. Accordingly, special attention is warranted for those aspects that differ from those of most other animals.

Skeletal System

One of the unique aspects of the internal anatomy of turtles is their skeletal system.

As with most other vertebrates, turtles have both axial and appendicular skeletons. The skull, vertebral column and ribs form the axial skeleton, while the shoulder girdle, pelvic girdle and limbs comprise the appendicular skeleton.

However, in turtles, the ribs are fused to form the shell. Unlike other vertebrates, whose pelvic and hip girdles are located *outside* the rib cage, turtles carry these bones *inside* their rib cage. While this arrangement helps to protect these areas from damage, it limits the mobility of most turtles.

Softshell turtles actually have reduced skeletons relative to those of most other turtle species. In effect, this has allowed them to exchange some of the protection other turtles enjoy for maneuverability and speed that are among the most impressive of any turtle species.

Digestive System

The digestive system of softshell turtles is similar to that of other turtles, and, to a lesser extent, vertebrates in general.

Just inside the mouth likes the esophagus, which transports food to the stomach. From here, food passes through the small and then large intestines before being expelled from the vent.

The pancreas and spleen lie close to the stomach, while the gallbladder attaches to the liver, just as it does in most other vertebrates.

Circulatory and Pulmonary System

In general, the circulatory and pulmonary systems of turtles are similar to those of other reptiles.

Turtles inhale and exhale through their mouth or nose, while the trachea carries air to and from two lungs. Because the turtle's shell is (at least partially) rigid, which prevents the ribs from moving (which would pump air into and out of the lungs), turtles have a collection of membranes and connective tissues that attach to the distal ends of the lungs. When these connective tissues contract and relax, the lungs empty and fill with air.

Like many other reptiles, turtles have three-chambered hearts, which feature two atria and a single ventricle. One atrium accepts oxygenated blood from the lungs, while the other atrium receives oxygen-poor blood from the body.

Both atria pump blood into a single ventricle, which then pumps the blood into the rest of the body. Normally, as in many other reptiles, this means that the turtle's body receives a combination of oxygen-rich and oxygen-poor blood. However, turtles have a primitive septum (wall) in their ventricle, which partially prevents the mixing of the two types of blood.

Accordingly, turtles have a slightly more efficient cardiovascular system than lizards and snakes do.

Urinary System
Softshell turtles filter waste products from their bloodstream via their paired kidneys. They then store these waste products in the urinary bladder. These waste products are released primarily in the form of urea.

Turtles have a renal portal blood system, which means that the blood traveling through the rear half of the turtles' body is filtered by the kidneys before making it to the front half of the body. This has important implications in turtle medical care; medications cannot be injected into the rear half of the body, as they kidneys will filter the medications before they can circulate widely.

Reproductive System
Turtle fertilization occurs internally, so they must mate to reproduce.

Males have a single intromittent organ (penis), making them similar to crocodilians and birds, but very different from snakes and lizards, who possess paired reproductive organs (termed hemipenes).

The penis of male turtles is held inverted, inside the tail base. During mating attempts, the penis everts and protrudes outside of the vent.

Females have a pair of ovaries, in which eggs form and reside; and a pair of oviducts, which accept the eggs once they are released. The eggs join the sperm inside the oviducts, where they continue to develop.

Before the eggs are deposited, calcium and other minerals coat the surface of the developing embryos, thus giving rise to the eggshell.

Like females of many other species, softshell turtles can retain sperm from a single mating for many months and possibly longer.

Chapter 2: Softshell Turtle Biology and Behavior

Softshell turtles exhibit a number of biological and behavioral adaptations that allow them to survive in their natural habitats. In many ways, softshell turtles employ strategies and possess adaptations that are quite different from those of other turtles.

Metabolism and Digestion

Like most other non-avian reptiles, softshell turtles have slow metabolisms. This not only means that it takes them longer than many other animals to process their food, but also, they require less food to remain alive.

In general, ectothermic ("cold-blooded") animals require about one-fifth to one-twentieth of the food that similarly sized endothermic ("warm-blooded") animal do. It also means that while softshell turtles do not normally fast for long periods of time like snakes do, they can live for much longer without food than a comparably sized endothermic animal can.

This trade off occurs because ectothermic animals – like softshell turtles – do not use calories to heat their bodies as mammals and birds do. Instead, they rely on outside heat sources, such as the sun, to keep their body at the appropriate temperature.

Growth Rate and Lifespan

The growth rate of softshell turtles varies in relation to the amount of food they can acquire. Accordingly, because they benefit from essentially unlimited food, captive softshell turtles grow much more quickly than their wild counterparts. In fact, wild softshell turtles may fail to grow for several years if they are unable to obtain sufficient food.

Like most other reptiles, softshell turtles grow quickly while they are young, but their growth rate slows considerably once they reach maturity. Most softshell turtles mature over a period of 3 to 7 years.

Foraging Behavior

Softshell turtles are incredibly skilled swimmers, so they can catch some prey species by pursuing them through the water. However, most prey is probably captured via ambush hunting techniques.

Often, they do so by burying their bodies under a thin layer of sand or mud, with only their head protruding. They'll remain like this for extended periods of time, waiting to snatch any unsuspecting animal that swims too closely.

Softshell turtles may also consume carrion when the opportunity arises, or search for mollusks and crustaceans amid underwater cover or vegetation.

Diel and Seasonal Activity

Softshell turtles are primarily diurnal animals, meaning that they are active during the day and sleep during the night. They may be active at any hour of the day or night in captivity, but true nocturnal activity is relatively rare. At night, most softshell turtles lie along the bottom of their tank, often buried under a layer of substrate.

Softshell turtle seasonal patterns vary greatly from one location to the next. Subspecies living in northern areas typically hibernate throughout the long winter. Conversely, those living in southern regions may remain active all year long.

Generally speaking, the duration of the active season decreases with increasing latitude.

Defensive Strategies and Tactics

Despite their large size and prickly temperaments, softshell turtles try to avoid encounters with predators whenever possible. Their cryptic colors and patterns help to accomplish this goal, but they are also very skilled swimmers, which helps them to flee from danger when the need arises. Few predators are capable of capturing them as they slice through the water.

However, when cornered or unable to escape a predator, softshell turtles will fight savagely. They may bite or scratch at the perceived threat, and some individuals may void the contents of their cloaca when frightened.

Mature softshell turtles occasionally fall prey to humans, canids and felids, but alligators are probably their most important predators. Hatchling and juvenile softshell turtles, on the other hand, are vulnerable to a wide variety of predators in their natural habitats. Some of their predators include birds, raccoons, opossums, wading birds and snakes.

Reproduction

Male softshell turtles begin courting and attempting to mate with females during the spring. Egg deposition begins shortly thereafter and can continue through the summer.

Females can store sperm for several years, which allows them to deposit eggs for several years after an initial mating. Once it is time to deposit the eggs, females may travel very long distances to find nesting locations. Preferred sites usually feature a sandy substrate and ample insolation.

Females will dig their nests several inches deep and cover them thoroughly after depositing the clutch. The females will have no contact with the young (except through happenstance) after this point.

Chapter 3: Classification and Taxonomy

Scientists place species in a multi-tiered classification scheme to help facilitate communication and to signify the evolutionary relationships among closely related taxa.

Understanding this classification scheme can help you better understand softshell turtles and their place in the tree of life.

Reptiles in the Tree of Life

For decades, scientists have debated the definition of the term "reptile." (Anderson, 2003)

On the one hand, lizards, snakes, crocodiles and turtles are all instantly recognizable as reptiles, thanks to their scaly skin and other traits.

However, the reptile evolutionary lineage, when considered in its entirety, must also include dinosaurs, and their direct descendants, the birds.

Regardless of which definition taxonomists ultimately agree upon, the history of the group is relatively well known. Reptiles first evolved approximately 300 million years ago, when they branched off the amphibian family tree.

This lineage produced an amazing array of species, including dinosaurs, mosasaurs and pterodactyls, as well as the ancestors of modern snakes, lizards and turtles. Most of these lineages died out almost completely, but a few managed to survive to the present day. Currently, reptiles are represented by the following groups:

- Crocodilians
- Squamates (snakes and lizards)
- Sphenodontids (tuataras)
- Testudines (turtles)
- Birds

Testudines in the Tree of Life

All living turtles can trace their origin back to the same ancestral species, meaning that all living turtles are part of the same evolutionary lineage. Scientists call such lineages monophyletic.

Two different names are commonly used to refer to the group, including "testudines" and "chelonians". While modern looking turtles likely appeared in the Jurassic period, a few primitive turtle fossils have been discovered from Triassic period deposits.

These turtles, which lived about 220 million years ago, differed greatly from modern turtles. Not only did they lack the proper shell of modern chelonians, they had teeth embedded in their upper and lower jaws.

Because of the unique body plan of testudines (a term that refers to all the various types of turtles, including marine, terrestrial and freshwater species), scientists have long debated the group's placement within the tree of life.

Those swayed by morphological data believe that turtles are most closely aligned with Lepidosaurs (a group that includes snakes, lizards and tuataras). In part, this is based on the holes (fenestra) in the skulls of ancient turtles, which resemble those present in the skulls of lizards and snakes.

However, recent genetic studies of a wide variety of species has shed light on the placement of turtles within the tree of life, as well as the placement of individual species within the turtle umbrella. (Crawford, 2012)

According to this new research, turtles are the sister group to archosaurs (a group that includes crocodilians, birds and several extinct groups, such as non-avian dinosaurs). Lepidosaurs are the sister group to the ancestor of both archosaurs and testudines (a group named the archelosauria).

This means that the closest living relatives of turtles are crocodilians and birds, rather than snakes and lizards. Nevertheless, the two groups diverged from a common path hundreds of millions of years ago. So, while the two groups are each other's closest living relatives, they are not especially closely related.

As of November 2016, scientists currently recognize 346 living testudines, but this number fluctuates as new species are discovered, different species are synonymized and subspecies are elevated to the level of full species.

Softshell Turtles in the Tree of Life

Herpetologists categorize all living turtles in the order Testudines. The first major division in this lineage occurs between those turtles who withdraw their neck in a lateral plane (called the sub-order Pleurodira), and those who draw their neck back in a vertical plane, called the sub-order Cryptodira.

Like most other living turtles, softshell turtles are members of the sub-order Cryptodira. Within this sub-order, softshell turtles are members of the family Trionychidae.

Some of the most important genera in the family include:

Apalone
The genus *Apalone* contains three recognized species: the spiny softshell (*Apalone spinifera*), Florida softshell (*Apalone ferox*) and smooth softshell (*Apalone mutica*). These are all native to North America, and represent the most commonly kept species in captivity.

Pelochelys
Pelochelys contains three species, which are not suitable for captivity, yet still deserve mention as they are thought to be the largest softshell turtles in the world. Cantor's giant softshell turtle (Pelochelys cantorii) is the largest known species, reaching 6 feet (1.8 meters) in shell length. The New Guinea softshell turtle (*Pelochelys bibroni*) is the second largest species, reaching about 3 feet (1 meter) in length. The Northern New Guinea softshell turtle (*Pelochelys signifera*) is rather poorly known, and smaller than the other two.

Pelodiscus
The genus *Pelodiscus* contains four living species, all of which hail from Asia. Most are rather poorly known and represented in captivity, but the Chinese softshell turtle (*Pelodiscus sinensis*) is farmed in Asia as a food source and frequently seen in the pet trade.

Chapter 4: The Softshell Turtle's World

To maintain a softshell turtle successfully, you must understand the animal's native habitat and provide a reasonable facsimile of it.

Range and Habitat

Although all softshell turtles are aquatic animals, who live in various water bodies, the different species live in many different geographical locations.

Three species are native to North America, but others inhabit Asia and Africa. Most prefer water with some current, but some live in ponds, swamps and small lakes. All species prefer waters that feature soft, sandy or muddy bottoms, in which they'll spend long periods of time hiding. Most prefer areas that have a moderate amount of vegetation.

Most softshell turtle species live in tropical or subtropical zones, although several species do penetrate beyond the 40th parallel in both the North America and east Asia.

Natural Diet

Without exception, softshell turtles are opportunistic carnivores who consume a variety of different aquatic and terrestrial creatures. The only vegetation they consume is swallowed inadvertently, often during the process of eating a prey animal.

Young softshell turtles primarily feed on small invertebrates and fish, but as they mature, other animals are incorporated into the diet. Some of the most common animals eaten include:

- Fish
- Frogs
- Salamanders
- Crayfish
- Freshwater Shrimp
- Freshwater Crabs
- Clams
- Aquatic Snails
- Rodents
- Snakes
- Turtles
- Birds

Natural Predators

Softshell turtles are slightly more vulnerable to predation than many other turtles are, but they use their speed, agility and biting ability to help keep them safe from most threats.

As with virtually all other species, the young are disproportionately more vulnerable to predation than the adults are. Young softshells are likely at risk from every small to medium predator lurking on or around the water, including:

- Snakes
- Large Frogs
- Large Crayfish
- Wading Birds
- Fish

- Large Turtles
- Raccoons
- Opossums
- Sea Gulls
- Crocodilians

By contrast, adult softshell turtles likely have relatively few predators. Large cats, various canines, crocodiles and alligators are likely the only predators beside humans that routinely prey upon them.

PART II: SOFTSHELL TURTLE HUSBANDRY

Once equipped with a basic understanding of what softshell turtles *are* (Chapter 1 and Chapter 3), where they *live* (Chapter 4), and what they *do* (Chapter 2) you can begin learning about their captive care.

Animal husbandry is an evolving pursuit. Keepers shift their strategies frequently as they incorporate new information and ideas into their husbandry paradigms.

There are few "right" or "wrong" answers, and what works in one situation may not work in another. Accordingly, you may find that different authorities present different, and sometimes conflicting, information regarding the care of these turtles.

In all cases, you must strive to learn as much as you can about your pet and its natural habitat, so that you may provide it with the best quality of life possible.

Chapter 5: Softshell Turtles as Pets

Caring for any animal is a profound responsibility that requires both the means and the desire to provide it with a high quality of life.

It is imperative that potential keepers understand what is involved in caring for a softshell turtle, before adding one to their home and family.

Softshell Turtle Suitability

When provided with suitable housing, care and veterinary attention, softshell turtles often thrive in captive environments. The many softshell turtles living happy and healthy lives in zoos, museums, educational institutions and private homes around the world demonstrate this clearly.

However, softshell turtles present a number of husbandry challenges, which can often stymie novice keepers. In fact, they are not suitable pets for many would-be keepers. Softshell turtles require elaborate housing, including heating and lighting fixtures, substrates and hiding places. Additionally, their relatively large size (even males are relatively large by pet turtle standards) complicates and increases the cost of their care.

Softshell turtles also live long lives, and few keepers are prepared to provide them with the proper care for multiple decades. They require daily maintenance and unusual food sources (including live insects or other feeder animals).

Softshell turtles also suffer from a few common health problems, making it important for turtle owners to continue to learn about their pets and work closely with their veterinarian.

Captive bred animals typically harbor fewer parasites than their wild-caught counterparts do, but many animals in the pet trade are wild caught. This not only means that these animals may harbor parasites or disease, but it places pressure on wild populations.

While they are not for everyone, experienced keepers, with the resources, desire and dedication befitting such amazing animals, can successfully maintain these turtles in captivity.

What You'll Need

To keep a softshell turtle as a pet, you must provide it with all of its needs. This includes:

- A suitable enclosure full of clean water
- High-quality water filter
- Appropriate substrate
- Basking platforms
- Heating and lighting equipment
- Monitoring equipment (thermometers, etc.)
- Husbandry tools (tongs, etc.)
- Transport containers
- Cage cleaning equipment and supplies

While every situation is different, a couple of fair scenarios are laid out in the following chart. These represent the initial costs of becoming a softshell turtle owner; they do not address on-going costs such as food and veterinary care.

Costs of Captivity

Inexpensive Option

Hatchling Softshell Turtle	$25 (£16)
Large Plastic Storage Box	$50 (£32)
Entry-level Filter	$50 (£32)
Heating and Lighting Equipment	$100 (£64)
Digital Indoor-Outdoor Thermometer	$15 (£9)
Infrared Thermometer	$35 (£22)
Basking Platform	$20 (£13)
Miscellaneous Equipment	$25 (£16)
Total	$320 (£204)

Moderate Option

Sub-Adult Softshell Turtle	$50 (£32)
Large Pond Liner	$100 (£64)
Mid-Level Filter	$100 (£64)
Heating and Lighting Equipment	$100 (£64)
Digital Indoor-Outdoor Thermometer	$15 (£9)
Infrared Thermometer	$35 (£22)
Cage Furniture	$30 (£19)
Miscellaneous Equipment	$25 (£16)
Total	$455 (£290)

Premium Option

Albino Softshell Turtle	$500 (£400)
Custom Outdoor Enclosure	$1,000 (£640)
Premium Filter	$300 (£195)
Digital Indoor-Outdoor Thermometer	$15 (£9)
Infrared Thermometer	$35 (£22)
Basking Platforms	$50 (£32)
Miscellaneous Equipment	$25 (£16)
Total	$1,925 (£1,534)

Myths and Misunderstandings

Before going further, it is important to distinguish between some of the myths and facts surrounding softshell turtles and their care.

Myth: Softshell turtles need friends or they will get lonely.

Fact: Although softshell turtles occasionally interact in the wild (obviously, they must during breeding attempts), they often act aggressively toward other turtles, even other softshell turtles. Accordingly, it is usually wise for keepers – particularly novice keepers – to keep them singly.

Myth: Turtles grow in proportion to the size of their cage and then stop.

Fact: Reptiles do no such thing. Healthy softshell turtles reach at least 10 inches or so in length regardless of the size of their enclosure, and healthy females may reach two or three times this size. Placing them in a small cage in an attempt to stunt their growth is an **unthinkably cruel practice**, which is more likely to sicken or kill your pet than stunt its growth.

Myth: Softshell turtles can survive on any food you give them.

Fact: Diet is one of the most important components of softshell turtle husbandry and you must select food items very deliberately. In addition to providing your turtle with high-quality food, it is wise to rotate food items regularly to avoid deficiencies. Dietary problems often become quite serious before obvious symptoms appear and they can be very difficult – sometimes impossible – to rectify.

Myth: Reptiles have no emotions and do not suffer.

Fact: While turtles have very primitive brains, and do not have emotions comparable to those of higher mammals, they absolutely can suffer. Always treat reptiles with the same compassion you would offer a dog, cat or horse.

Myth: Softshell turtles are ferocious animals who will readily bite their owner.

Fact: While softshell turtles are typically foul tempered, they can adapt to routine interaction with their keeper. Understand that these turtles are not "mean" or "vicious," they've just evolved to respond vigorously when they feel threatened.

Acquiring a Softshell Turtle

Now that you have decided to get a softshell turtle, and you understand the care it requires, it is time to find your pet. Modern reptile enthusiasts can acquire softshell turtles from a variety of sources, each with a different set of pros and cons.

PRO TIP: It is easy to get over excited about the potential of a new pet, which can lead to hasty decisions and regret. Take your time and select the perfect turtle for you. You will have your pet for the next several decades; you can take a few weeks to find the ideal companion.

Pet Stores

Pet stores are a common source for many beginning turtle keepers, but they are not always the best place to purchase a new pet.

The benefits of shopping at a pet store are that they usually have all of the equipment to care for your new turtle, including cages, heating devices and food items. You will usually be able to inspect the animal up close before purchase. In some cases, you may be able to choose from more than one specimen.

Many pet stores provide health guarantees for a short period, which provides you with some recourse if your new pet turns out to be ill. However, pet stores are retail establishments, and as such, you will pay more than you will from a breeder.

The drawbacks to purchasing a turtle from a pet store relate to the amount of expertise and knowledge of the staff. While some pet stores concentrate on reptiles and may have a staff capable of providing them with proper care, many turtles languish while living in pet stores. Pet stores do not often know the pedigree of the animals they sell, nor are they likely to know the turtle's date of birth, or other pertinent information.

It is also worth considering the increased exposure to pathogens that pet store animals endure, given the constant flow of animals through the facility.

Reptile Expos

Reptile expos *can be* excellent places to acquire new animals. Reptile expos often feature resellers, breeders and retailers in the same room, all selling various types of turtles and other reptiles.

Often, the prices at such events are quite reasonable and you are often able to select from many different turtles. However, reptile expos are not without their problems.

For example, if you have a problem with your new pet, it may be difficult to find the seller after the event is over. Do not assume that a given vendor is skilled and reputable just because they have paid for a table at the event. Use your critical thinking skills and research the vendor as much as possible (you can likely do an internet search from your phone while you are speaking with him or her), before making the purchase.

Breeders
Breeders are the best place for most novices to shop for turtles. Breeders generally offer unparalleled information and support after the sale. Additionally, breeders often know the species well, and are better able to help you learn the husbandry techniques for the animal.

The disadvantage of buying from a breeder is that you must often make such purchases from a distance, either by phone or via the internet. Breeders often have the widest selection of turtles, and are often the only place to find rare forms and truly spectacular specimens.

Classified Advertisements
Newspaper and website classified advertisements sometimes include listings for turtles. While individuals, rather than businesses generally post these, they are viable options to monitor. Often, these sales include the turtle and all of the associated equipment, which is convenient for new keepers. However, be careful to avoid purchasing someone else's "problem" (i.e. a sick or maladapted turtle).

Selecting Your Turtle
Not all turtles are created equally – you want to be careful in selecting the best specimen you can find. While you can consider color or other aesthetic qualities in your selection process, they should be minor concerns. Only select turtles that appear healthy.

Health Checklist
Never purchase a softshell turtle displaying any of the following signs or symptoms:

- Lumps, swellings or ulcers on the skin or shell
- Puffy or closed eyes
- Limb or tail deformations

- Overgrown beak
- Discharge from the eyes
- Discharge from the nostrils or mouth
- Discharge from the vent

Additionally, healthy softshell turtles should move easily, and be alert and active. If the turtle is small enough to be held, it should feel heavy for its size; sick turtles often feel very light.

The Sex
In most cases, males are preferable to females for captive maintenance. Males not only remain smaller than females do, they will typically experience fewer health concerns.

Additionally, by selecting a male, you will not have to deal with the problem of egg deposition. Female turtles – even those who are not housed with males – may produce eggs. If they cannot find a suitable egg deposition site, they may become egg bound. This can necessitate expensive and invasive surgeries, or lead to death.

Captive Bred Vs. Wild Caught
For a litany of reasons, captive bred softshell turtles are unquestionably superior pets to wild caught specimens.

Whereas captive bred individuals are usually healthy and well-adapted to the captive environment, wild caught individuals are often heavily parasitized, stressed, malnourished and dehydrated. Many bear the scars typical of a life spent dealing with the threats of the wild.

While it is possible for experienced keepers to overcome these challenges, and nurse these individuals back to health, novices will usually struggle.

Another problem with wild caught turtles is that these animals have been removed from the wild. This places wild populations – and in some cases, entire taxa -- at risk of extinction.

Unfortunately, many softshell turtles available in the market are wild caught juveniles or young adults, but captive bred animals can be found with a bit of effort.

Chapter 6: Providing the Captive Habitat

The first thing that you need to keep a softshell turtle as a pet is the enclosure – it is the defining characteristic of captivity!

Over the years, keepers have used a wide variety of enclosure types, each of which offers different benefits and drawbacks. Some keepers prefer inexpensive, functional enclosures and place a premium on things like cost, durability and ease of maintenance, while other keepers desire to build the most visually impressive habitat possible. Still others may design an enclosure well suited for captive reproduction.

Similarly, keepers differ on the space requirements of turtles; some find relatively modest cage sizes to be sufficient, while others prefer to provide their turtles with larger accommodations.

Regardless of which side of the spectrum you fall on, you must always provide your pet with an enclosure that is large enough to meet the turtle's basic needs – minimally including sufficient room to establish thermal gradients, permit exercise and allow mental stimulation for the animal.

As you proceed, consider all of the variables facing you and your pet, and design a habitat that best fits your circumstances.

Indoor or Outdoor?

The first major decision you must make with respect to the enclosure is its location. Specifically, you must decide whether you wish to keep your turtle indoors or outdoors. Both approaches have their merits and challenges, and you must decide which approach is best for your pet.

Because of their lightning needs, most turtles thrive best when kept outdoors and allowed to bask in unfiltered, natural sunlight. While reptile lighting systems have come a long way in the last few decades, no lightbulb will ever be able to produce the same quality and intensity of light as the sun does.

Softshell turtles will likely thrive outdoors in any place that is home to wild-living softshell turtles. This includes most of the United States as well as areas with similar climates, such as the warmer portions of

Europe. Alternatively, if you live in areas with *very* cold winter temperatures, indoor maintenance will be required.

However, even if the local climate is suitable for softshell turtles, outdoor housing is not without its drawbacks – particularly as it relates to immature specimens.

Small softshell turtles are at greater risk to predators and less tolerant of temperature extremes than the adults are. They are also more difficult to monitor in outdoor enclosures (unless the enclosures are very small), which presents additional challenges for the keeper.

Considering all the various factors, the best path forward is to keep your pet indoors while it is young, and then move to an outdoor husbandry regimen, once it is large enough to be safe from predators and better able to tolerate temperature extremes.

Safety for Outdoor Turtles
Despite their strong jaws and aquatic habits, softshell turtles can end up as prey for a variety of predators. The list of potential suburban predators that may prey upon softshell turtles includes:

- Snakes
- Herons
- Raccoons
- Foxes
- Feral cats
- Feral dogs
- Coyotes
- Hawks
- Owls
- Minks
- Weasels
- Crows
- Ravens
- Opossum

Accordingly, it is imperative that you take steps to keep small individuals safe if you choose to house your turtle outdoors.

Each of these predators relies on a different skill set to find and capture prey. This means that you may need to employ multiple safety features to protect your pet.

For example, a smooth wall 4 to 6 feet (1.2 to 1.8 meters) high surrounding the habitat will likely keep out most snakes and feral dogs, but it will do very little to keep out hawks, owls or crows. Conversely, a mesh cover with an open weave may prevent birds from dining on your turtle, but it will do little to keep out snakes.

Digging predators – dogs, weasels, foxes and others – also represent a tunneling threat; so, you must construct the wall so that it penetrates below ground level for a distance of at least 1 to 2 feet (30 to 60 centimeters).

And while it is not pleasant to think about, humans may steal or harm your pet. Locks and security systems will reduce the chances of people accessing the enclosure, but they provide no guarantees.

Although they are not true "predators" in the strictest sense of the word, rodents may gnaw on sleeping turtles of all sizes, so you must take all reasonable measures to exclude them from the habitat too.

Types of Enclosures

Softshell turtles are almost entirely aquatic; so, the bulk of their habitat should hold water. However, all softshell turtles require a place to exit the water and bask, and females require an area containing a soft substrate that they can use for egg deposition.

Many commercial options are suitable for small softshell turtles, including aquaria and plastic turtle tubs. You can also repurpose items such as plastic storage boxes, small swimming pools, pond liners and cattle troughs for your turtle's habitat -- virtually any smooth-sided, non-toxic, durable container will work.

However, relatively few commercial options are appropriate for large softshell turtles. A handful of commercial turtle tubs and aquaria are marketed for "large" turtles, but most keepers will find it necessary to construct a custom enclosure of some kind.

If you live in a pet- and child-free home, you can forgo a lid for the cage, but if small creatures have access to the habitat, a lid is necessary.

Materials for Custom Enclosures

You'll have to think carefully about the materials you use while constructing a custom enclosure. The bulk of the habitat must hold water, so you'll have to ensure it can do so safely.

Glass, plastic and metal are the most common choices for building custom enclosures, although you can also use cement if you prefer. It is also possible to use wood, provided that you seal it well enough to hold water.

Each material has benefits and drawbacks. For example, glass is heavy and fragile, but it provides excellent visibility of your pet. Metal is extremely durable, but this is a material that requires special tools and knowledge to use.

Plastic is relatively durable, inexpensive and light, but it will become scratched over time. This can present challenges with keeping the tank clean, and scratches look terrible in transparent plastics (such as Plexiglas).

Enclosure Size and Layout

In most cases, rectangular cage designs are superior to square or round cage designs. This is because the rectangular layout allows you to create a more effective thermal gradient in a given amount of space than a square or round layout does.

Additionally, rectangular enclosures provide a longer distance that the animal can travel before reaching a barrier, which is likely to promote better health and well-being.

Nevertheless, some keepers have had great success with cages of all shapes and configurations. As long as the turtle's needs are met, any configuration will work. To some extent, you will have to customize the enclosure to suit your home, given the scale of the enclosure.

Softshell turtle tanks should have a large footprint, but they need not be very deep, unless you live in a particularly cold region. One to two shell-lengths worth of water depth is sufficient.

A sloped bottom is ideal, especially if there are plateaus at different depths. For example, you may construct a tank with a 4-square-foot area at about 3 feet (90 centimeters) of depth, connected to another, similar area at about 1 foot (30 centimeters) of depth. A sloped bottom should connect the two.

The proper size for a to three turtle's cage is a subject of great debate. Many authorities present conflicting suggestions. In all cases, suggested cage sizes should be considered the minimum acceptable. Larger cages are almost always better.

Some experienced keepers advocate that enclosure should be five times the turtle's length long, three times the turtle's length wide, and at least two times the turtle's length deep. "Length" in these contexts refers to the length of the turtle's shell when measured in a straight line.

In other words, by this guideline, a 10-inch-long softshell turtle requires a 50-inch-long, 30-inch-wide, 20-inch deep enclosure. Likewise, a 2-

inch-long yearling would require a cage 10-inches-long, 6-inches-wide and 4-inches deep.

Other authorities recommend arbitrary tank sizes. Such keepers typically recommend starting with a 20- to 40-gallon aquarium, and moving up to 100-gallon aquariums upon maturity. However, it is important to understand that the capacity of the tank varies with the layout.

While a low-profile tank that contains 100 gallons of water may be large enough for a small adult, a typical 100-gallon aquarium sold in pet stores has been designed for fish. Accordingly, such tanks have a very small footprint, but greater depth. Such cages are wholly inappropriate for large softshell turtles.

The Zoological Association of America requires turtles to have enclosures with an area equal to at least five times the length of the turtle's shell by two times the turtle's shell width. The pool area should be at least two times the shell length by two times the shell width. Additionally, an area of dry land equal to the size of the turtle's shell is required.

Chapter 7: Water Quality and Filtration

As with fish, aquatic turtles require clean, healthy water to remain healthy. While most turtles are not as sensitive to water conditions as fish are, poor water quality can lead to health problems.

Proper filtration and periodic water changes will keep most of the relevant water quality parameters within tolerances, but you may need water conditioners and other chemicals to keep the pH correct and to alleviate any chlorine or chloramine in the water.

Important Aspects of Water Quality

Be sure that you address each of the following water quality issues to keep your turtle's tank water clean.

- **Chlorine / Chloramine** – Chlorine and chloramine are used as antibacterial agents in tap water. You can remove or neutralize both agents with water conditioners sold at pet stores.

- **Ammonia / Nitrites / Nitrates** – Ammonia levels in the tank will rise over time, as your turtle releases waste into the water. Ammonia is toxic, but fortunately, nitrifying bacteria can convert ammonia into nitrates. Nitrates are also toxic, but different bacteria can convert nitrates into nitrites, which are relatively harmless. The bacteria necessary to complete the process will form naturally on your filter media. However, it is important to monitor the levels of ammonia, nitrates and nitrites to keep the water as healthy as possible; you can do this with a water test kit.

- **pH** – Softshell turtles generally prefer water that is slightly acidic. Most keepers aim for a pH of about 6.5 when maintaining softshells. A water test kit will allow you to monitor the pH. Your local pet store will have products available to adjust the pH in either direction, as necessary.

Filtration

Unless you plan to perform water changes several times each week, a high-quality water filter is necessary for softshell turtle maintenance.

Modern filters treat the water in three different ways. The first stage in the process, called mechanical filtration, removes the particulate matter from the tank. The second stage uses bacteria living on the filter media to convert ammonia and its derivatives into safer substances – this is called biological filtration. Finally, the water passes through an activated carbon filter, which bonds with most chemicals passing through it. This step is referred to as chemical filtration.

The style of the water filter is not terribly important; some keepers prefer canister-style filters, while others prefer units that hang on the back of the aquarium. Either style will work – the important consideration is the capacity of the filter.

Filters are rated for varying quantities of water. For example, you may see filters rated for 100-gallon aquariums and others rated for 20-gallon aquariums. These ratings work well for aquariums containing fish, but because turtles create a considerable amount of waste, it is wise to select a filter rated for two to three times the size of your turtle's tank. In other words, if your pet lives in a 50-gallon habitat, purchase a filter rated for 100- or 150-gallon aquariums.

You will need to clean the filter unit regularly to keep it working at peak efficiency. Avoid using any chemicals to do so; instead, simply rinse the unit and filter cartridges with water. Be sure to use "dirty" tank water to rinse the biological filter cartridge, as chlorinated water will kill the bacteria.

Water Changes

While your filter will help keep the tank water clean, few models are effective enough to keep the water clean without a little help. This help comes in the form of partial water changes.

To perform a partial water change, begin by preparing enough new water to replace about half of the water in the tank. Treat the water as necessary to remove or neutralize the chlorine or chloramine, and allow it to warm to room temperature. Then, remove and discard approximately half of the water in the tank. Finally, add the new water to the tank to complete the partial water change.

You can use a bucket to bail water from the turtle tank, but a siphon hose will make the project much easier. Complete a partial water change about once every week or two to keep the water clean and reduce the workload for the tank filter.

Chapter 8: Heating and Lighting

Ectothermic, or "cold-blooded," animals, such as softshell turtles, primarily heat their bodies via external sources, such as by basking in the sunlight or sitting on a warm rock.

When they cannot reach suitable temperatures, they cannot digest their food effectively, move as quickly as necessary or perform other behaviors and bodily functions.

This can lead the animal to become dormant, such as occurs during the winter; or, it can cause the animal to become ill. Therefore, to maintain any ectothermic animal, such as a softshell turtle, you must provide an enclosure with suitable temperatures.

Depending upon your local climate and the manner in which you house your turtle, you may need one or more heating devices as well as the necessary monitoring equipment. Additionally, you must arrange the heating equipment in such a way that you provide the captive with a range of temperatures.

Ideal Climate for Softshell Turtles

Softshell turtles have adapted to a variety of different climates across their wide range, but most individuals prefer the air temperatures in the high-70s Fahrenheit to the mid-80s Fahrenheit (25 to 30 degrees Celsius), and water temperatures in the mid-70s Fahrenheit (23 to 24 degrees Celsius). However, they also like to have access to a basking spot of about 88 degrees Fahrenheit (31 degrees Celsius). They will remain active at temperatures slightly outside this range, but extreme temperatures will cause them to seek shelter and become inactive.

In most situations, softshell turtles adjust their activity levels to match the climate. However, extended periods of time at suboptimal temperatures can affect their health of cause them to become dormant.

Temperatures can and should be allowed to drop slightly at night, just as they do in the wild. Mature turtles housed indoors can usually be allowed to cool to room temperature overnight, as long as they are allowed to warm up properly in the daytime.

Thermal Gradients

One of the most basic principles of animal husbandry is to provide captives with a range of conditions, from which they can choose which is the most comfortable.

For example, it is wise to provide all captives – particularly reptiles and other ectothermic critters, who modify their temperature behaviorally – with a range of temperatures in their enclosure.

Keepers call this practice establishing a *thermal gradient*. Creating a thermal gradient is fairly simple -- you just need to place the enclosure heat source(s) at one end of the cage. This way, temperatures will gradually fall with increasing distance from the heat source.

In the case of aquatic turtles, this means placing the basking lamp and the water heater (if necessary) on the same side of the enclosure. The areas closest to the heat sources provide warmth for the animal, while the far end of the cage serves as a cool retreat – intermediate temperatures allow your animal to fine-tune its internal temperature.

However, the temperatures of the enclosure need not be maintained in exactly this fashion; rather than a linear variation in temperatures, you can provide the turtle with several "zones" of different temperatures. This will also allow your pet to move about the enclosure and regulate his temperature.

Indeed, neat, linear gradients are not always feasible when maintaining turtles outdoors. You cannot move the sun, so you are limited to shading portions of the habitat to establish a range of temperatures.

Heating Devices

You can use any of several different types of heating devices. All have different pros and cons, which make a given device work in one scenario but not another.

CAUTION: Always use care when arranging and operating heating devices and follow all of the manufacturer's instructions.

It is generally ill advised to place heating devices outdoors, where they will be exposed to the elements. If the ambient temperatures are not high enough to keep your turtles healthy, they should be brought inside.

The Sun

If you plan to keep your softshell turtles outdoors, the sun will serve as your primary heating source. While the sun offers many benefits to both the keeper and the kept, it also provides unique challenges.

On the plus side, the sun provides the best spectrum of light possible for turtle maintenance, it is free and it requires no maintenance; but on the other hand, you have no control over this heat source.

At best, you can try to maximize the sun exposure of the enclosure by positioning it so that it catches the most hours of sunlight possible. You will still need to contend with overcast or rainy days, but, provided that these are not common, the occasional cool, dreary day will cause the turtles no harm.

Heat Lamps

Heat lamps are the most common type of heating device used by turtle keepers to provide basking spots.

When reptile keepers refer to a "heat lamp", they mean a portable light socket surrounded by a shroud. A variety of different bulbs can be screwed into the receptacle. For example, some keepers prefer to use regular, incandescent light bulbs, while others prefer mercury vapor bulbs.

It is easy to adjust the temperature underneath a heat lamp by either changing the distance between the light and the substrate or swapping out the bulb for a different wattage.

Ceramic Heat Emitters

Ceramic heat emitters are used in place of a light bulb in a heat lamp fixture. However, unlike a light bulb, ceramic heat emitters produce no light. They only produce heat, which emanates from the ceramic.

On the plus side, most manufacturers claim that ceramic heat emitters are much more efficient than light bulbs. Additionally, as they produce no light, they can be used to heat the enclosure at night, without disturbing your pet's circadian rhythms.

However, ceramic heat emitters also have negative characteristics. Because they produce no light, you cannot tell if it is on or not by looking at it. This can lead to injuries if you accidentally touch it while it is on.

Ceramic heat emitters are also rather expensive, although when the efficiency and lifespan of the device is taken into consideration, this difference may become insignificant.

Heat Tape

Heat tape is plastic-covered electrical wire that is designed to heat up when current is applied. Heat tape is not appropriate for creating a basking spot, but it may help to keep indoor enclosures at the desired level, when placed underneath the habitat. However, you must be sure to allow air to flow across the heat tape to prevent a dangerous buildup of heat.

Heat tape is largely inappropriate for beginning reptile keepers, as it must be wired by hand. You must use heat tape with a thermostat or rheostat to maintain the proper temperatures. If you do not, the heat tape will become much too hot and may cause a fire.

Care must be used when laying out heat tape, as improper placement can represent a fire hazard – always follow the manufacturer's instructions when assembling or using heat tape.

Heat Pads

Heating pads made for reptiles are generally constructed by enclosing a length of pre-wired heat tape in a plastic cover. Like heat tape, heat pads are not helpful for maintaining a basking spot, but they may help heat the substrate if placed below the cage. Be sure that the manufacturer's instructions permit this type of use before using a heat pad in this manner.

Heating pads should always be used with a thermostat or rheostat to maintain appropriate temperatures.

Heat Cables

Heat cables are long conducting wires that heat up when current is applied to them. Most heat cables are covered in plastic, which may or may not make them suitable for use outdoors or in situations in which they become damp.

Like heat tape or heating pads, you must use heat cables with a rheostat or, preferably, a thermostat.

Radiant Heat Panels

Radiant heat panels are similar to heating pads, except that they are designed to project heat rather than warm things that are in contact with the device. Additionally, radiant heat panels are usually placed on the ceiling or wall of an enclosure. This makes them very helpful for providing a basking spot.

Radiant heat panels often cost more than heat lamps do, but they provide safer, more controlled heat. However, radiant heat panels must be used with a thermostat to ensure they do not overheat.

Heated Rocks and Other Items
Heated rocks, branches, caves and other items were some of the earliest and most popular commercial heating devices for pet reptiles. They are made from a faux rock (or stick, etc.) and an internal heating element.

In previous decades, heated rocks garnered a bad reputation for burning reptiles. In some cases, this was due to faulty equipment, but in many others, it was due to keeper error.

These types of devices are not designed to raise the temperature of a pet reptile's habitat – they are merely designed to provide a localized basking spot. Unfortunately, many early keepers did not understand this, and so their pet reptiles wrapped tightly around these devices, while sitting in a woefully under heated cage.

Newer designs feature built-in rheostats or thermostats and are often constructed with better components. Nevertheless, they are inappropriate for turtles of any kind, and should be avoided.

Monitoring and Control Equipment
Maintaining an appropriate climate in your pet's enclosure often requires some trial and error, but this does not mean that you should blindly approach the task.

Instead, you must measure the cage temperatures, to ensure they are within the comfortable range for your pet.

Thermometers
Turtle keepers need two different types of thermometers to monitor their pet's environment properly: one to measure the ambient air and water temperatures and another to measure the surface temperatures of objects in the habitat.

Several different types of thermometers are appropriate for measuring the ambient air temperature, including analog and digital varieties. Often, digital, indoor-outdoor models are the best choice, as they feature a remote sensing probe. These probes allow you to monitor the temperature in two different portions of the habitat simultaneously, such as the basking spot and the deep water.

To measure the surface temperatures in the enclosure – such as the basking spot or the top of your pet's shell while he is under the basking spot – use an infrared, non-contact thermometer. Dedicated keepers often find these tools immensely valuable; invest in a quality unit, as you are likely to end up using it quite often.

Avoid the plastic, "stick-on" variety of thermometer often sold in pet stores.

Rheostats
Rheostats are akin to "volume controls" for heating devices. They work like lamp dimmer switches, as they reduce the amount of electricity reaching the heating device. This reduction in electricity reduces the amount of heat produced by the device.

Rheostats are helpful tools as they allow you to fine-tune the amount of heat supplied by a given device. However, you must still monitor the temperatures regularly, to ensure the cage temperatures stay within the desired range.

Thermostats
Thermostats are similar to rheostats, but they automatically adjust the amount of electricity reaching the heating device, in order to maintain a pre-selected temperature. Several different types of thermostats are available commercially.

Some work by simply switching the power to the heating device on and off. Others work by continually adjusting the amount of electricity reaching the device.

The former are called on-off thermostats while the later are termed pulse-proportional thermostats. On-off thermostats are only suitable for use with heat pads, radiant heat panels or heat tape.

While you must regularly check to ensure your thermostats are working, they are very helpful for maintaining proper cage temperatures, and they largely automate climate control.

Some thermostats feature a night-drop function, which allows you to program the unit to drop the temperatures by a preselected amount each night.

Thermostat Failure

Eventually, all thermostats will fail. Whether this occurs a week after you purchase the unit or 30 years from now remains to be seen, but you must prepare for the possibility.

In a worst-case scenario, thermostat failure can lead to the death of your animals.

You can provide yourself with some protection from thermostat failure by purchasing a high-quality unit, crafted from quality components. However, even expensive thermostats can fail.

Another option is to use two thermostats, wired in series. To accomplish this, you must set the primary thermostat to the preferred temperature range for your animal. You then attach a second thermostat behind the first. Set this thermostat to a few degrees higher than the primary thermostat.

This way, when the primary thermostat fails, the secondary thermostat will allow the temperature to rise a few degrees, but will prevent the habitat from becoming dangerously warm.

Differing Thermal Requirements

Like most other types of animals, small turtles are less tolerant of temperature extremes than large turtles are. In addition, because they have greater surface-to-volume ratios than larger turtles do, small individuals change temperatures much more quickly than their larger counterparts do.

Accordingly, it is wise to keep the maximum temperatures available to small turtles a few degrees below that provided to large individuals, and to keep the minimum temperatures a few degrees higher than those that are provided to large turtles.

Lighting

Most turtles require very specific lighting to remain healthy. Without it, pet turtles may develop shell irregularities, lose bone mass or suffer kidney failure, among other problems.

The easiest way to solve this problem is by maintaining your turtle outdoors. But this is not always possible, and is not ideal for young animals, who are vulnerable to predators.

Therefore, in lieu of natural sunlight, keepers should provide pet turtles with high quality, "full-spectrum" lighting. Full spectrum lighting refers to lights that produce not only visible light, but light in the UV portion of the range.

More specifically, turtles generally require lights that produce light in both the UVA and UVB portions of the range. UVA is defined as light between 320 and 400 nanometers, while UVB is defined as light between 290 and 320 nanometers.

UVC, which has wavelengths of between 100 and 290 nanometers, is destructive to cells, and is not produced by bulbs designed for reptile cages or general illumination.

UVA wavelengths have been shown to influence the vision and behavior of reptiles, and may play a role in food recognition. UVB wavelengths have widely been shown to allow reptiles to convert inactive vitamin D to the active form (Vitamin D3).

Vitamin D3 is crucial to the metabolism of calcium. When reptiles are deficient in vitamin D3, they tend to draw calcium from their bones. This leads to soft bones, and is termed metabolic bone disease. Often, the condition proves fatal, or becomes debilitating enough to require euthanasia. Once the symptoms of metabolic bone disease present themselves, the disease is often in an advanced state.

Most full spectrum lights are fluorescent bulbs. Both conventional and compact styles are available. Minimally, you must incorporate full spectrum bulbs over the basking site, but you can place them along the entire length of the enclosure if you prefer. However, if you choose to illuminate the entire tank with full-spectrum bulbs, be sure to offer the turtle refuges, where it can avoid the light.

The amount of UVB light emanating from the bulb dissipates rapidly with increasing distance from the lamp. This means that you must place the lights relatively close to the basking reptile – a maximum of about 12 inches (30 centimeters).

Full spectrum lights lose their ability to produce UVB over time, so you must replace them regularly. Follow the manufacturer's instruction regarding replacement schedule, but most lights last between 6 and 12 months.

Plug the full-spectrum lights into a lamp timer to keep your pet's photoperiod consistent. It is probably best to recreate the seasonal variation characteristic of the turtle's home range in captivity. However, some keepers have success by keeping their pets under a daylight variation pattern characteristic of the keeper's location.

Of course, if you maintain your turtles outdoors, you will have no control of the photoperiod.

Chapter 9: Substrate and Furniture

Now that you have decided what type of enclosure is right for you and your turtle, you can start placing the necessary items in the tank.

Most reptiles feel more secure in complex habitats than they do barren boxes with no visual barriers or items to investigate. However, you must strike a delicate balance between adding enough items to the enclosure to give your pet a sense of security and overcrowding the habitat, which makes maintenance more difficult and reduces the effective space available to your pet. Additionally, because softshell turtles frequently dig in the substrate, they'll often dislodge plants and other items in the cage. Accordingly, it is best to err on the minimalist side when decorating the habitat when keeping softshell turtles.

Substrates

The only appropriate substrates to use in softshell turtle habitats is smooth, fine-grained aquarium sand, or sand you have harvested from a nearby waterbody.

The sand will not only provide a place for the turtles to hide, it will also act as an exfoliant, and remove dead skin cells, algae and bacteria clinging to their shell.

Softshell turtles can temporarily be maintained in tanks with bare floors, but this is only acceptable for brief periods.

Furniture

The most important cage furniture for your softshell turtle is a secure, stable basking platform. You can make a basking platform out of a variety of different items or materials, including wooden branches, cork bark, large rocks or commercial platforms.

You can purchase the materials for a basking platform from a pet or craft store, or you can collect them yourself. Branches, for example, are easy to collect and can be used to create wonderful basking platforms.

If you decide to collect your own branches, try to use ones that are still attached to trees (always obtain permission first). Such branches are less likely to harbor insects or other invertebrate pests than fallen, dead branches will.

Most of the insects that infest wood will cause your turtle no harm, but they may release frass (insect droppings mixed with wood shavings) into the enclosure's water, causing the keeper more work. Theoretically, some of these insects may also damage your house, should they escape the cage, but this probably not something to lose sleep over.

Many different types of branches can be used to create a good basking platform. Most non-aromatic hardwoods suffice. See the chart below for specific recommendations.

Whenever collecting wood to be used in your turtle's enclosure, bring a ruler so that you can visualize how large the branch will be, once it is back in the cage. Leave several inches of spare material at the ends of the branches; this way, you can cut them to the correct length back home.

Always wash branches with plenty of hot water and a stiff, metal-bristled scrub brush to remove as much dirt, dust and fungus as possible before placing them in your turtle's enclosure. Clean stubborn spots with a little bit of dish soap, but be sure to rinse them thoroughly afterwards.

Some of the best tree species to use include those in the table below.

Recommended Species	Species to Avoid
Maple trees (*Acer* spp.)	**Cherry trees** (*Prunus* spp.)
Oak trees (*Quercus* spp.)	**Pine trees** (*Pinus* spp.)
Walnut trees (*Juglans* spp.)	**Cedar trees** (*Cedrus* spp., etc.)
Ash trees (*Fraxinus* spp.)	**Juniper trees** (*Juniperus* spp.)
Dogwood trees (*Cornus* spp.)	**Poison ivy / oak** (*Toxicodendron* spp.)
Sweetgum trees (*Liquidambar stryaciflua*)	
Crepe Myrtle trees (Lagerstroemia spp.)	
Tuliptrees (*Liriodendron tulipifera*)	
Pear trees (*Pyrus* spp.)	
Apple trees (*Malus* spp.)	
Manzanitas (*Arctostaphylos* spp.)	
Grapevine (*Vitis* spp.)	

Regardless of the material you choose to use, the platform must be roomy enough to accommodate the turtle (you'll need to add additional basking platforms or increase the size of the basking platform if you house more than one turtle in the enclosure). The platform must also be easy for the turtles to climb onto and it must be securely fastened in place, right under the heat and full-spectrum lamps. Do not allow the platform to simply float around the tank, as this makes it harder for the turtles to access and it may cause the platform to move away from the enclosure lights.

You can attach the branches to the enclosure walls in a variety of different ways. The branches should be held very securely, but you must be able to remove them periodically.

Closet rod holders are a popular choice for attaching suitably-sized branches to the cage walls, but they must not allow the branches to roll when the turtle climbs on the platform.

To keep them in a fixed position, small pegs can be placed on the branch ends that prevent them from rolling. Alternatively, branches with three or more ends can be used; three or more contact points will prevent the branch from spinning.

Some keepers use hooks and eye-screws to suspend their branches. This method allows for quick and easy removal, but it is only applicable for cages with walls that will accept and support the eye-screws, such as those built from plastic or wood.

It can be challenging to suspend branches in glass cages and aquaria. It is often necessary to use an adhesive to hold the supports securely to the cage walls. Be careful placing pressure on glass walls or panels, as they crack easily.

If the notion of gathering and arranging a collection of branches to build a platform does not appeal to you, you can consider using rocks to build a suitable platform.

Select the flattest rocks you can while doing so, so that the platform created will be very stable and safe – you don't want rocks falling inside the enclosure, as they could injure your turtles or puncture one of the side walls. It is probably best to cement the rocks together to help provide additional stability.

Of course, you can always avoid the need for a basking platform entirely if you create a "beach" instead. Many keepers prefer to go this route, as this also provides an easy way to include an egg-deposition chamber in the enclosure.

Aside from a basking platform (if required), softshell turtles do not require very much cage furniture. Just add a few logs and rocks to the cage so they will have things to explore and easy avenues for accessing the land or basking area.

However, you'll need to be careful that you do not restrict your turtle's activity by overcrowding the tank with rocks and sticks. It is also important to ensure such items are securely fastened, so your turtle does not topple them and damage the tank or injure itself.

Plants

Plants are another great addition to a softshell turtle enclosure. In addition to providing hiding places for your turtle, plants increase the amount of dissolved oxygen in the water. Plants also compete with algae for nutrients, which can help to reduce algae blooms. Some keepers prefer to use artificial plants rather than live plants, as they require less care and frequent replacement.

Relatively little research has been conducted on the safety of different aquatic plants, but the following plants are likely safe for your pet. When in doubt, it is always wise to consult with your veterinarian before adding live plants to the enclosure.

- Water hyacinth
- Duckweed (*Lemna minor*)
- Water lettuce
- Water weed (*Elodea* spp.)
- (*Egeria densa*)
- Java fern (*Microsorium pteropus*)
- Java moss (*Vesicularia dubyana*)
- Hornwort (*Ceratophyllum demersum*)
- Red Ludwigia (*Ludwigia repens*)

Many of these plants can be floated, attached to rocks or left in their original containers.

Chapter 10: Maintaining the Captive Habitat

Now that you have acquired your turtle and set up the enclosure, you must develop a protocol for maintaining his habitat. Most illnesses in captive reptiles spring from inappropriate husbandry (particularly the failure to keep the habitat suitably clean), so be vigilant about maintaining the habitat to avoid such problems.

In addition to designing a husbandry protocol, you must embrace a record-keeping system to track your pet's growth and health.

Maintenance Schedule

Try to establish a regular maintenance routine. Some tasks are necessary on a daily basis, while other tasks can be performed less frequently.

Daily

- Visually inspect the habitat and turtle, looking for any problems with the habitat or health concerns.
- Be sure that the habitat remains secure and that your pet cannot escape.
- Ensure that the temperatures in the habitat are within the appropriate range.
- Clean the habitat, removing any uneaten food or other such items from the enclosure.

Weekly

- Perform a full water test to ensure that the water chemistry is within the correct range.
- Physically inspect your turtle, looking for signs of illness or injury.
- Inspect any spots in the cage where debris and bits of organic matter can lurk, such as under plants or decorations.
- Perform a 25% to 50% water change.

Monthly

- Break down the aquarium filter, clean all the internal components and replace it. Place the biological filter inside the tank water during the cleaning process to avoid killing off the beneficial bacteria.

- Replace plants or cage furniture as necessary.

- Weigh and measure your turtle. This is particularly important with young turtles, so that you can monitor their growth. If your turtle is mature, and healthy, you can weigh and measure it less frequently.

- Scrape away any algae growing on the tank.

Annually

- Change full-spectrum bulbs in indoor cages (some bulbs require replacement every 6 months – consult the manufacturer's instructions).

- Inspect all of the electrical cords, light fixtures and all other equipment for signs of wear.

- Completely break down the cage (as much as is possible), clean the furniture, hoses, filters, thermometers and any other items present.

Chemicals & Tools

A variety of chemicals and tools are necessary for reptile care. Save yourself some time by purchasing dedicated cleaning products and keeping them in the same place that you keep your tools.

Scrub Brushes or Sponges

It helps to have a few different types of scrub brushes and sponges on hand for scrubbing and cleaning different items. Use the least abrasive sponge or brush suitable for the task to prevent wearing out cage items prematurely. Do not use abrasive materials on glass or acrylic surfaces. Steel-bristled brushes work well for scrubbing coarse, wooden items, such as branches.

Spatulas and Putty Knives

Spatulas, putty knives and similar tools are often helpful for cleaning reptile cages. They allow you scrape away dirt and other materials, instead of trying to dissolve them with harsh chemicals.

Small Vacuums
Small, handheld vacuums are very helpful for sucking up the dust left behind from substrates. They are also helpful for cleaning the cracks and crevices around the cage doors. A shop vacuum, with suitable hoses and attachments, can also be helpful, if you have enough room to store it.

Additionally, wet-dry vacuums are also helpful for removing small amounts of water from your turtle's tank, or cleaning up spilled water.

Steam Cleaners
Steam cleaners are very effective for sterilizing cages and durable cage props after they have been cleaned. In fact, steam is often a better choice than chemical disinfectants, as it will not leave behind a toxic residue. Never use a steam cleaner near your turtle, the plants in his cage or any other living organisms.

Soap
Use a gentle, non-scented dish soap. Antibacterial soap is preferred, but not necessary. Always ensure that any items that have been washed with soap are rinsed completely before returning them to the tank. Soap residue may irritate your turtle's eyes, nose, mouth and skin.

Bleach
Bleach (diluted to one-half cup per gallon of water) makes an excellent disinfectant. Be careful not to spill any on clothing, carpets or furniture, as it is likely to discolor the objects.

Always be sure to rinse objects thoroughly after using bleach and be sure that you cannot detect any residual odor. Bleach does not work as a disinfectant when in contact with organic substances; accordingly, items must be cleaned before you can disinfect them.

Veterinarian Approved Disinfectant
Many commercial products are available that are designed to be safe for their pets. Consult with your veterinarian about the best product for your situation, its method of use and its proper dilution.

But note that you should always avoid cleaners that contain phenols, as they are extremely toxic to some reptiles. In general, do not use household cleaning products to avoid exposing your pet to toxic chemicals.

Keeping Records

It is important to keep records regarding your pet's health, growth and feeding, as well as any other important details. In the past, reptile keepers would do so on small index cards or in a notebook. In the modern world, technological solutions may be easier. For example, you can use your computer or mobile device to keep track of the pertinent info about your pet.

You can record as much information about your pet as you like, and the more information to you record, the better. But minimally, you should record the following:

Pedigree and Origin Information
Be sure to record the source of your turtle, the date on which you acquired him and any other data that is available. Breeders will often provide customers with information regarding the sire, dam, date of birth, weights and feeding records, but other sources will rarely offer comparable data.

Feeding Information
Record the date of each feeding, as well as the type of food item(s) offered. It is also helpful to record any preferences you may observe or any meals that are refused.

It is also wise to record the times you supplement the food with calcium or vitamin powders, unless you employ a standard weekly protocol.

Weights and Length
Because you look at your pet frequently, it is difficult to appreciate how quickly he is (or isn't) growing. Accordingly, it is important to track his size diligently.

Weigh your turtle with a high quality digital scale. It is often easiest to use a dedicated "weighing container" with a known weight to measure your turtle. This way, you will not have to keep the animal stationary on the scale's platform – you can simply place him in the container and place the entire container on the scale. Subtract the weight of the container to obtain the weight of your pet.

You can measure your turtle's length as well, but it is not as important as tracking his weight. Usually, it is easier and safer to just measure your turtle's straight-line shell length, as opposed to trying to measure his total length, including his head and tail.

Maintenance Information
Record all of the noteworthy events associated with your pet's care. Whenever you purchase new equipment, supplies or caging, note the date and source. This not only helps to remind you when you purchased the items, but it may help you track down a source for the items in the future, if necessary.

Breeding Information
If you intend to breed your turtle, you should record all details associated with pre-breeding conditioning, cycling, introductions, matings and egg deposition.

Record all pertinent information about any resulting clutches as well, including the number of viable eggs, as well as the number of unhatched and unfertilized eggs (often called "slugs" by reptile keepers).

Record Keeping Samples
The following are two different examples of suitable recording systems.

The first example is reminiscent of the style employed by many with large collections. Because such keepers often have numerous animals, the notes are very simple, and require a minimum amount of writing or typing.

The second example demonstrates a simple approach that is employed by many with small collections (or a single pet): keeping notes on paper. Such notes could be taken in a notebook or journal, or you could type directly into a word processor. It does not matter *how* you keep records, just that you *do* keep records.

ID Number:	44522	Genus: Species/Sub:	Apalone ferox	Gender: DOB:	Male 3/20/15	CARD	#2
6.30.15 6 minnows	7.03.15 5 crickets	7.08.15 5 minnows	7.14.15 25% Water change	7.17.15 3 worms			
7.01.15 4 minnows	7.05.15 5 minnows	7.09.15 2 roaches	7.15.15 2 newborn mice	7.19.15 Cleaned filter			
7.02.15 3 shrimp	7.06.15 6 crickets	7.12.15 8 minnows	7.16.15 4 minnows				

Date	Notes
4-22-13	Acquired "Pancake" the Florida softshell turtle from a breeder named Mark at the in-town reptile expo. Mark explained that Pancake's scientific name is Apalone ferox. Cost was $50. Mark said he purchased the turtle in March, but he does not know the exact date.
4-23-13	Pancake spent the night in the container I bought him in. I purchased a small plastic storage box cage, a heat lamp and a thermometer at the hardware store, and I ordered a non-contact thermometer online. I am ordering a full-spectrum light too so I can make sure he stays healthy!
4-27-13	Pancake was really hungry! He ate 6 minnows in about 10 minutes.
4-28-13	I fed Pancake 2 crickets and a couple of earthworms today. He is so cute when he is trying to catch them!
4-30-13	I gave Pancake 6 minnows today, but I think I'm going to need to give him more from now on.
5-2-13	Fed Pancake a dozen minnows today and he ate each one! At this rate, I may just start breeding minnows at home to save money.

Chapter 11: Feeding Softshell Turtles

Diet is one of the most important aspects of softshell turtle maintenance, and good health requires a diet that mimics their natural diet. Fortunately, this is fairly easy to accomplish with softshell turtles.

Softshell turtles are almost exclusively carnivorous. They may occasionally ingest a bit of vegetation, but they primarily feed upon live animals, including fish, reptiles, amphibians and invertebrates.

Although the diet of the various subspecies varies slightly, most will thrive on a relatively similar collection of items. Try to provide your pet with the broadest selection of acceptable foods possible.

Some of the most important food sources are detailed below.

Invertebrates

Invertebrates make up a large percentage of the diet of young softshell turtles, and they can make up a large portion of the diet of adults in some habitats.

Many invertebrates are available commercially, although it is possible to collect others from places in which it is legal to do so. Some of the most commonly fed invertebrates include:

- Crickets
- Crayfish
- Crabs
- Mealworms
- Superworms
- Wax Worms
- Silkworms
- Roaches
- Grasshoppers
- Slugs
- Snails
- Earthworms

Vertebrates

Wild softshell turtles eat a variety of vertebrate prey in the wild, however, only a few such animals are appropriate to feed captives. These include:

- Rodents
- Live Minnows
- Chicks
- Ducks

Wild softshell turtles also consume snakes, lizards, turtles, salamanders, frogs and other creatures swimming alongside them or lurking near the water's edge. However, these are generally inappropriate food sources for captive animals.

Commercial Foods
Despite their preference for live, mobile foods, softshell turtles can often be trained to eat pelleted foods.

A variety of commercially produced foods are available for pet turtles. The nutritional quality of these foods varies from one manufacturer to the next, so be sure to scrutinize the nutritional information provided closely.

While commercial foods make a valuable component of a healthy softshell turtle's diet, they should only represent a small portion of it, with fish and invertebrates making up the bulk.

Offering Food to Your Softshell Turtle
There are two different ways to provide prey or pellets to your turtle.

Small, live creatures and pellets can simply be released into the tank. Just be sure that they are all eaten or removed before they can reproduce (especially important with snails) or cause other harm to the tank or its inhabitant. Allowing your pet to chase down small fish or pellets will help to provide mental stimulation and a small amount of exercise.

Large items, such as prekilled rodents, chicks or large fish, should be offered via tongs or long forceps. By slowly moving the food item in front of the turtle's mouth, you can "animate" it, and entice your softshell turtle to strike.

Use extreme care when feeding softshell turtles, particularly large specimens.

Feeding Frequency and Quantity
In addition to feeding your turtle a diverse selection of healthy foods, you must feed your pet the correct amount of food to ensure good health.

Softshell turtles likely feed every day in the wild, and a similar feeding strategy makes sense for captives. Offer your pet as much food as he or she can eat in about 5 to 10 minutes and then carefully remove the uneaten portion. Nevertheless, you can skip a day every once in a while, without harming our pet.

The exact caloric needs of your pet will vary based on its gender, age, size, activity level and the foods you offer. Accordingly, you must monitor your pet to provide the ideal amount of food.

Track your turtle's growth to help ensure he receives enough food. Young animals should grow at a slow, yet consistent rate; while adults may eventually cease growing, they should maintain their body weight.

Vitamin and Mineral Supplements

Many keepers add commercially produced vitamin and mineral supplements to their turtle's food on a regular basis. In theory, these supplements help to correct dietary deficiencies and ensure that captive turtles get a balanced diet. In practice, things are not this simple.

While some vitamins and minerals are unlikely to build up to toxic levels, others may very well cause problems if provided in excess. This means that you cannot simply apply supplements to every meal – you must decide upon a sensible supplementation schedule.

Additionally, it can be difficult to ascertain exactly how much of the various vitamins and minerals you will be providing to your turtle, as most such products are sold as fine powders, designed to be sprinkled on feeder insects. This is hardly a precise way to provide the proper dose to your pet, and the potential for grossly over- or under-estimating the amount of supplement delivered is very real.

Because the age, sex and health of your turtle all influence the amount of vitamins and minerals your pet requires, and each individual product has a unique composition, it is wise to consult your veterinarian before deciding upon a supplementation schedule.

Chapter 12: Interacting with Your Softshell Turtle

You must be sure that your interactions with your turtle are safe and positive for all parties involved. Contact with a large predator (such as yourself) may cause the turtle stress, which can lead to illness and maladaptation. Additionally, improper handling can cause your pet to suffer serious injuries – and in the case of large softshell turtles, *you* are also at risk of serious injuries.

In general, this means that you should avoid most unnecessary physical contact with your pet. However, you need to observe your turtle for signs of illness regularly, and this will occasionally necessitate directly handling or manipulating the animal.

Handling Your Turtle
The best way to hold hatchling softshell turtles is by placing your index finger on top of the animal's carapace and placing your thumb under its plastron. Do not pinch the shell too firmly, as young turtle shells lack the rigidity of adult shells. Keep your fingers well back from the turtle's head.

The best way to hold large softshell turtles is by using both hands, and gripping the rear margin of the shell, near the legs. This is not easy to do, and you'll be subject to the rear claws, which will usually be flailing around in an attempt to scratch you.

Never use a turtle's tail to support its bodyweight, as it can lead to spinal injuries.

Transporting Your Turtle
From time to time, it will be necessary to transport your pet. When doing so, you must keep the turtle protected from injury, within the appropriate temperature range and protected from sources of stress.

The best way to do so is by placing your turtle in a plastic storage box, filled with a soft layer of newspaper or mulch. Opaque boxes will keep your turtle calmer, while transparent boxes will allow you to observe the animal without opening the lid. Keep the substrate very damp, as softshell turtles dehydrate quickly.

Be sure to drill a few ventilation holes on each of the container's vertical sides so that your pet can breathe easily. When drilling the holes, drill from the inside of the tub toward the outside, to prevent any sharp edges from contacting your turtle.

Hygiene

Turtles often carry various strains of *Salmonella* bacteria, as well as other harmful pathogens. While these bacteria rarely cause illness in the turtles, they can make humans – particularly those with compromised immune systems – very ill. In tragic cases, death can result from such infections.

Accordingly, it is imperative to employ sound hygiene practices when caring for a pet turtle. In general, this means:

- Always wash your hands with soap and warm water following any contact with your pet, the enclosure or items that have contacted either.

- Never wash turtle cages, furniture or tools in sinks or bathtubs used by humans.

- Never perform any husbandry tasks in kitchens or bathrooms used by humans.

- Keep high-risk individuals, such as those who are less than 5 years of age, elderly, pregnant or otherwise immunocompromised, away from captive turtles and their habitats.

Chapter 13: Common Health Concerns

Like many other turtles, softshell turtles are remarkably hardy animals, who often remain healthy despite their keeper's mistakes. In fact, most illnesses that befall pet turtles result from improper husbandry, and are therefore, entirely avoidable.

Nevertheless, like most other reptiles, softshell turtles often fail to exhibit any symptoms that they are sick until they have reached an advanced state of illness. This means that prompt action is necessary at the first hint of a problem. Doing so provides your pet with the greatest chance of recovery.

While proper husbandry is solely in the domain of the keeper, and some minor injuries or illnesses can be treated at home, veterinary care is necessary for many health problems.

Finding a Suitable Vet

While any veterinarian – even one who specializes in dogs and cats – may be able to help you keep your pet happy, it is wise to find a veterinarian who specializes in treating reptiles. Such veterinarians are more likely to be familiar with your pet species and be familiar with the most current treatment standards for reptiles.

Some of the best places to begin your search for a reptile-oriented veterinarian include:

- Veterinary associations

- Local pet stores

- Local colleges and universities

It is always wise to develop a relationship with a qualified veterinarian before you need his or her services. This way, you will already know where to go in the event of an emergency, and your veterinarian will have developed some familiarity with your pet.

When to See the Vet

Most conscientious keepers will not hesitate to seek veterinary attention on behalf of their pet. However, veterinary care can be expensive for the keeper and stressful for the kept, so unnecessary visits are best avoided.

If you are in doubt, call your veterinarian and explain the problem. He or she can then advise you if the problem requires an office visit or not.

However, you must always seek prompt veterinary care if your pet exhibits any of the following signs or symptoms:

- Traumatic injuries, such as lacerations, burns, broken bones, cracked shells or puncture wounds

- Sores, ulcers, lumps or other deformations of the skin

- Intestinal disturbances that do not resolve within 48 hours

- Drastic changes in behavior

- Inability to deposit eggs

Remember that reptiles are perfectly capable of feeling pain and suffering, so apply the golden rule: If you would appreciate medical care for an injury or illness, it is likely that your pet does as well.

Common Health Problems

The following are some of the most common health problems that afflict turtles – especially softshell turtles. Be alert for any signs of the following maladies, and take steps to remedy the problem.

Respiratory Infections

Respiratory infections are some of the most common illnesses that afflict turtles and other captive reptiles.

The most common symptoms of respiratory infections are discharges from the nose or mouth; however, lethargy, inappetence and behavioral changes (such as basking more often than normal) may also accompany respiratory infections.

Myriad causes can lead to this type of illness, including communicable pathogens, as well as, ubiquitous, yet normally harmless, pathogens, which opportunistically infect stressed animals.

Your turtle may be able to fight off these infections without veterinary assistance, but it is wise to solicit your vet's opinion at the first sign of illness. Some respiratory infections can prove fatal and require immediate attention.

Your vet will likely obtain samples, send off the samples for laboratory testing and then interpret the results. Antibiotics or other medications may be prescribed to help your turtle recover, and your veterinarian will likely encourage you to keep the turtle's stress level low, and ensure his enclosure temperatures are ideal.

In fact, it is usually a good idea to raise the temperature of the basking spot upon first suspecting that your turtle is suffering from a respiratory infection. Elevated body temperatures (such as those that occur when mammals have fevers) help the turtle's body to fight the infection, and many will bask for longer than normal when ill.

Metabolic Bone Disease
Metabolic bone disease (MBD) is a complicated phenomenon that befalls turtles who are provided with insufficient calcium or insufficient amounts of the active form of vitamin D (D3), which is necessary for calcium utilization.

Many keepers supplement their turtle's food items with calcium powders to help avoid MBD, but it is important to consult with your veterinarian to devise a suitable supplementation schedule, as providing too much calcium can be just as problematic as providing too little.

A balanced diet will provide your turtle with plenty of inactive vitamin D. To allow your pet to convert this into the active form, you must provide it with exposure to ultraviolet radiation (specifically UVB). This can be accomplished either by housing your turtle outdoors and allowing them to bask in natural sunlight, or by illuminating their enclosure with full spectrum lights that produce light in the UVB portion of the spectrum.

When deprived of proper lighting, the calcium levels in the turtle's blood fall. This causes the turtle's body to draw calcium from the bones (including the shell) to rectify the problem.

As calcium is removed from the bones, they become soft and flexible, rather than hard and rigid. This can lead to broken bones or disfigurement, which can leave your turtle unable to eat, walk or swim.

Advanced cases of MBD are rarely treatable, and euthanasia is often the only humane option. However, when caught early and treated aggressively, some of the symptoms of the disease can be stopped. Accordingly, it is of the upmost importance to seek veterinary care at the first sign of MBD.

Shell Rot

Shell rot is a catchall term for a variety of maladies related to a turtle's shell. Shell rot normally takes the form of lesions or ulcers; sometimes, a small amount of fluid may leak from the wounds.

Shell rot may occur because of a systematic infection or as a local phenomenon. Bacteria or fungi may be the primary cause of the problem, or injuries may provide an opportunity for pathogens to colonize the tissues.

Shell rot is usually treatable with prompt veterinary care, so always see your veterinarian at the first sign of problems.

Parasites

Parasites are rare among captive-bred turtles, but poor husbandry can cause them to become a problem. Parasites rarely become problematic for wild turtles, unless they become injured, stressed or ill.

Most internal parasites cause intestinal problems, such as runny or watery stools, vomiting or decreased appetites. Your veterinarian can collect blood or stool samples from your turtle, analyze them to determine what parasites, if any, are present, and prescribe medications to clear the infestation. Often, multiple treatments are necessary to eradicate the parasites completely.

External parasites afflict softshell turtles on occasion, usually in the form of leaches. If you cannot remove the leaches easily, solicit your vet's help to avoid damaging your turtle's shell.

Anorexia

Softshell turtles are normally ravenous eaters, who rarely pass up the chance to consume calories. However, they may refuse food if ill, if kept in suboptimal temperatures (including seasonally cool temperatures, such as occur during the winter) or are preoccupied by breeding.

Refusing a meal or two is not cause for alarm, but if your turtle refuses food for longer than this, be sure to review your husbandry practices. If the turtle continues to refuse food without an obvious reason for doing so, consult your veterinarian.

Injuries

Despite their protective shells turtles can become injured in myriad ways, including battles with cagemates, overly zealous breeding attempts, or by sustaining burns from heaters. While turtles are likely to heal from most minor wounds without medical attention, serious wounds will necessitate veterinary assistance.

Your vet will likely clean the wound, make any repairs necessary (shell patches, sutures, etc.) and prescribe a course of antibiotics to help prevent infection. Be sure to keep the enclosure as clean as possible during the healing process.

Egg Binding
Egg binding occurs when a female is unable or unwilling to deposit her eggs in a timely fashion. If not treated promptly, death can result.

The primary symptoms of egg binding are similar to those that occur when a gravid turtle approaches parturition. Egg bound turtles may dig to create an egg chamber or attempt to escape their enclosure. However, unlike turtles who will deposit eggs normally, egg bound turtles continue to exhibit these symptoms without producing a clutch of eggs.

As long as you are expecting your turtle to lay eggs, you can easily monitor her behavior and act quickly if she experiences problems. However, if you are not anticipating a clutch, this type of problem can catch you by surprise.

Prolapse
Prolapses occur when a turtle's intestines protrude from its vent. This is an emergency situation that requires prompt treatment. Fortunately, intestinal prolapse is not terribly common among turtles.

You will need to take the animal to the veterinarian, who will attempt to re-insert the intestinal sections. Sometimes sutures will be necessary to keep the intestines in place while the muscles regain their tone.

Try to keep the exposed tissue damp, clean and protected while traveling to the vet. It is likely that this problem is very painful for the animal, so try to keep its stress level low during the process.

Quarantine
Quarantine is the practice of isolating animals to prevent them from transferring diseases between themselves.

If you have no other pet reptiles (particularly turtles), quarantine is unnecessary. However, if you already maintain other turtles (especially other softshell turtles) you must provide all new acquisitions with a separate enclosure.

At a minimum, quarantine all new acquisitions for 30 days. However, it is wiser still to extend the quarantine period for 60 to 90 days, to give yourself a better chance of discovering any illness present before exposing your colony to new, potentially sick, animals. Professional zoological institutions often quarantine animals for six months to a year. In fact, some zoos keep their animals in a state of perpetual quarantine.

Hygiene

Reptiles can carry *Salmonella* spp., *Escherichia coli* and several other zoonotic pathogens. Accordingly, it is imperative that you use good hygiene practices when handling reptiles.

Always wash your hands with soap and warm water each time you touch your pet, his habitat or the tools you use to care for him. Antibacterial soaps are preferred, but standard hand soap will suffice.

In addition to keeping your hands clean, you must also take steps to ensure your environment does not become contaminated with pathogens. In general, this means keeping your turtle and any of the tools and equipment you use to maintain his habitat separated from your belongings.

Establish a safe place for preparing his food, storing equipment and cleaning his habitat. Make sure these places are far from the places in which you prepare your food and personal effects. Never wash cages or tools in kitchens or bathrooms that are used by humans.

Always clean and sterilize any items that become contaminated by the germs from your turtle or his habitat.

Chapter 14: Breeding Softshell Turtles

Many – if not most – turtle keepers are eventually bitten by the captive breeding bug. Determined to produce a clutch of adorable hatchlings, these keepers acquire specimens of each sex and begin waiting for eggs.

This is a natural progression for keepers, and, when carried out in responsible fashion, breeding can be beneficial for the species, as captive breeding projects help alleviate pressure on wild populations.

However, irresponsible breeders often cause serious problems for the hobby.

Such breeders often set out with the explicit goal of profiting from their turtles, rather than enjoying their pets in their own right. This ensures failure for the vast majority of people that try to breed turtles for profit.

Pre-Breeding Considerations

Before you set out to breed softshell turtles, consider the decision carefully. Unfortunately, few keepers realize the implications of breeding their turtles before they set out to do so.

Ask yourself if you will be able to:

- Provide adequate care for a pair of adult turtles
- Provide the proper care for the female while gravid
- Afford emergency veterinary services if necessary
- Incubate the eggs in some type of incubator
- Provide housing for the hatchlings
- Provide food for the hatchlings
- Dedicate the time to caring for the hatchlings
- Find new homes for the hatchlings

If you cannot answer each of these questions affirmatively, you are not in a position to breed softshell turtles responsibly.

Legal Issues

Before deciding to breed turtles, you must investigate the relevant laws in your area. Some municipalities require turtle breeders to obtain licenses, insurance and permits, although others do not.

Finally, be aware that it is illegal to buy or sell turtles with carapaces less than 4 inches in length in the United States, except for educational or scientific purposes. This is a particularly important consideration when breeding relatively small turtles, because you may need to house them for some time, while waiting for them to attain the minimum size necessary.

Sexing Softshell Turtles

If, after considering the proposition carefully, you decide to breed softshell turtles, you will need at least one sexual pair of animals. To be sure that you have a sexed pair, you must be able to distinguish one sex from the other.

While it is difficult to identify the sex of young softshell turtles, it is relatively easy to distinguish between the sexes by the time they are 3 to 4 inches in length.

The best way to distinguish the sex of a softshell turtle is by observing its tail. Males have longer, thicker tails than females do, and the vent is usually positioned more distally in males than it is in females.

Mature females are easily recognized by their size, which is typically much greater than that of mature males.

Pre-Breeding Conditioning

Once you have obtained a sexual pair, you must begin conditioning them for breeding. This is important because animals that are not in very good condition may not be able to handle the rigors of cycling and breeding.

Take the turtles to visit your veterinarian, who will be able to ascertain their health status. Some veterinarians may only perform a visual inspection, but others may collect biological samples for additional testing.

If your vet determines that your turtles are not healthy, take whatever steps are recommended to rectify the problem before commencing breeding trials.

Once you are certain that your turtles are in good health, it is time to initiate your breeding protocols.

Cycling

Cycling is a term used to describe the practice of providing captive reptiles with an annual variation in temperature (or other factors, such as photoperiod). The concept seeks to mimic the natural seasonal cycle and synchronize the reproductive cycle of the reptiles in question.

For example, to cycle softshell turtles, the keeper may reduce the number of hours the basking lights are turned on, which will reduce the temperatures and photoperiod, causing the turtles to "feel" like they do in the winter. After four to eight weeks of these low temperatures, the basking light will be turned on for increasingly longer periods.

In some species, proper cycling appears to be necessary for successful reproduction in captivity, while other species reproduce quite successfully with no variation in temperature or any other factor.

Wild softshell turtles generally breed in the early spring through the summer, but captive individuals may breed at any time of the year.

Groupings and Housing

Most keepers prefer to keep the sexes separate for most of the year, and only introduce them to each other during breeding trials.

One of the benefits to keeping the sexes segregated is that it often results in vigorous courting and breeding by the males. As they say, absence makes the heart grow fonder. Additionally, singular maintenance reduces the likelihood of injuries and stress for both occupants.

While keeping softshell turtles in separate enclosures may be ideal, few keepers can devote enough space for multiple enclosures, and males are rarely reticent to breed (in fact, the opposite problem – continued, non-stop breeding – is often the problem). Instead, most keepers maintain breeding pairs together all year long.

It is important to use large enclosures when keeping animals in groups.

Gravid

Shortly after successful copulation, suitably healthy females become gravid. Unlike many other reptiles, turtles do not offer very many signs to indicate their reproductive condition.

Manual palpation, which is a common method for determining the reproductive condition of many other reptiles, is rarely helpful with turtles. In fact, attempting to feel a female's eggs with your fingers may cause them to rupture. Accordingly, it is wise to avoid the practice entirely. Instead, the best clues lie in the female's behavior.

Many gravid softshell turtles bask for longer periods of time, and begin eating very little food as their eggs develop and take up more space in their body cavity. They may also begin to explore their surroundings and look for a suitable place to dig their eggs.

Nevertheless, the only way to be certain that your turtle is gravid is by having your veterinarian perform an x-ray. This will not only verify that she is holding eggs, but it will allow you to know approximately how many eggs she is carrying.

Egg Deposition

As the time for egg deposition nears, the female will become increasingly restless. She may pace for long periods of time or even look for a way to escape from the enclosure.

At this point, the female is seeking out a place to dig a nest and deposit her eggs. Hopefully, you have designed the enclosure so that such a place is always available, but, if you have not, you must provide her with a place she finds suitable.

Typically, softshell turtles look for a warm, sunny area, with a sandy substrate suitable for nest construction. They prefer an area of exposed dirt, rather than having to dig through grass or vegetation.

Ideally, the egg-deposition site should have a footprint of at least two to three times the size of the turtle's shell and contain substrate as deep as the turtle's shell is long.

If your female does not find the provided site to her liking, you will need to tweak it until she feels comfortable. This can mean loosening the substrate, compacting the substrate, providing a greater depth of substrate or moving the egg deposition site to another location in the enclosure.

This is often a challenging component of turtle breeding, and even highly experienced zookeepers occasionally have problems devising a suitable egg-laying site.

If your turtle cannot find a suitable place to lay her eggs, she may scatter the eggs in the enclosure or retain them internally. Usually, these outcomes lead to health problems for the female, such as dystocia (egg binding).

Assuming that your turtle finds the egg deposition area suitable, she will eventually crawl into it, dig a small depression and fill it with about

6 to 30 eggs. After completing the process, she will cover the hole and leave the area. It can be very difficult to locate a nest site afterwards, so do your best to mark the location during, or immediately after, parturition.

Note that softshell turtles are often extremely shy during egg deposition, so do your best to stay out of sight and allow her to complete the process in private.

Egg Incubation

Keepers employ any of several different strategies for incubating softshell turtle eggs. No one method is "correct," although artificially incubating the eggs in a climate-controlled container usually leads to the greatest success.

The least labor-intensive approach for those housing softshell turtles outdoors is to leave the eggs where they are and let them incubate naturally. After all, softshell turtles have been incubating their eggs in just this way for millions of years.

However, doing so is unlikely to lead to a high rate of success, as you have little control over the temperatures of the mass. Additionally, the eggs may be vulnerable to predators, including rodents or fire ants, if the turtles are housed outside.

If you would prefer more control of the incubation process, you can excavate the egg chamber, remove the eggs and place them in a climate-controlled incubator for the remainder of their development.

Use great care when excavating the egg chamber to prevent damaging the eggs. Once you have accessed the eggs, mark the top of each with a graphite pencil. This will allow you to maintain the correct orientation when transferring the eggs to the incubator; inverting the eggs can cause the embryos to drown.

Avoid separating any eggs that have adhered to each other. While it is often possible to do so without damaging the eggs, such attempts should be left to those who have considerable experience incubating reptile eggs.

Egg Boxes

Egg boxes are small plastic storage boxes designed to hold the eggs inside the incubator. While their use is not always necessary in the strictest sense, they make it easier to maintain the climate surrounding the eggs.

Virtually any type of small plastic storage box will suffice, but consider a few things before selecting your egg boxes:

1. Be sure to select boxes that are tall enough to contain 1 or 2 inches (2.5 to 5 centimeters) of incubation media as well as the eggs, which will rest on top of the media (partially buried).

2. Whenever possible, select transparent egg boxes so that you can observe the eggs without having to open them.

3. If possible, select boxes with domed lids, which will help prevent condensation from dripping on the eggs.

You will need to make two small holes (approximately one-quarter-inch or one-half centimeter in diameter) in each box to allow for air exchange inside the egg boxes.

Some breeders prefer to monitor the temperature of the egg boxes, while others prefer to monitor the temperature of the incubator. Either method will work, although if you desire to measure the temperatures inside the egg boxes, you will need to drill additional holes to accept a temperature probe.

You can select relatively large egg boxes so that they will accommodate large clutches, or you can use relatively small egg boxes, so that you can split up the clutch into several different sub groups.

Incubation Media

Several different incubation media are appropriate for egg incubation. Soil, soil and sand mixtures and vermiculite are some of the most common choices by breeders. Vermiculite works for a wide variety of reptile eggs, as it is quite easy to attain a suitable moisture level.

The substrate not only provides a protective cushion that supports the eggs, but it also provides moisture, which will keep the relative humidity of the egg box high. This will prevent the eggs from desiccating.

Too much humidity or dampness, however, can have a negative effect on the eggs, so it is important to keep enough water in the egg boxes, but not too much.

Many keepers strive to maintain humidity levels of 80 percent in the egg chamber, but others simply watch the eggs and adjust the humidity accordingly. If the eggs begin to exhibit wrinkles, they are drying out and more water is necessary. Conversely, if they begin to swell or exude fluid, the humidity should be lowered.

Some authorities recommend specific ratios of water and vermiculite, but as vermiculite absorbs water from the air, it is impossible to know how saturated the vermiculite was when you started.

Accordingly, the best approach is to judge the moisture with your hands. Beginning with dry vermiculite, slowly add water while stirring the mixture. The goal is to dampen the vermiculite just enough that it clumps when compressed in your hand. However, if water drips from the media when you squeeze it, the vermiculite is too damp.

The Incubator

You can either purchase a commercially produced incubator or construct your own. However, most beginning breeders are better served by purchasing a commercial incubator than making their own.

Commercial Incubators

Commercial egg incubators come in myriad styles and sizes. Some of the most popular models are similar to those used to incubate poultry eggs (these are often available for purchase from livestock supply retailers).

These incubators are constructed from a large foam box, fitted with a heating element and thermostat. Some models feature a fan for circulating air; while helpful for maintaining a uniform thermal environment, models that lack these fans are acceptable.

You can place an incubation medium directly in the bottom of these types of incubators, although it is preferable to place the media (and eggs) inside small plastic storage boxes, which are then placed inside the incubator.

These incubators are usually affordable and easy to use, although their foam-based construction makes them less durable than most premium incubators are.

Other incubators are constructed from metal or plastic boxes; feature a clear door, an enclosed heating element and a thermostat. Some units also feature a backup thermostat, which can provide some additional protection in case the primary thermostat fails.

These types of incubators usually outperform economy, foam-based models, but they also bear higher price tags. Either style will work, but, if you plan to breed turtles for many years, premium models usually present the best option.

Homemade Incubators
Although incubators can be constructed in a variety of ways, using many different materials and designs, two basic designs are most common.

The first type of homemade incubator consists of a plastic, glass or wood box, and a simple heat source, such as a piece of heat tape or a low-wattage heat lamp. The heating source must be attached to a thermostat to keep the temperatures consistent. A thermometer is also necessary for monitoring the temperatures of the incubator.

Some keepers make these types of incubators from wood, while others prefer plastic or foam. Although glass is a poor insulator, aquariums often serve as acceptable incubators; however, you must purchase or construct a solid top to retain heat.

Place a brick on the bottom of the incubator, and place the egg box on top of the brick, so that the eggs are not resting directly on the heat tape. The brick will also provide thermal mass to the incubator, which will help maintain a more consistent temperature.

The other popular incubator design adds a quantity of water to the design to help maintain consistent temperatures and a higher humidity. To build such a unit, begin with an aquarium fitted with a glass or plastic lid.

Place a brick in the bottom of the aquarium and add about two gallons of water to it; ideally, the water level should stop right below the top of the brick.

Add an aquarium heater to the water and set the thermostat to the desired temperature. Place the egg box on the brick, insert a temperature probe into the egg box and cover the aquarium with the lid (you may need to purchase a lid designed to allow the cords to pass through it).

This type of incubator works by heating the water, which will in turn heat the air inside the incubator, which will heat the eggs. Although it can take several days of repeated adjustments to get these types of incubators set to the exact temperature you would like, they are very stable once established.

Incubation Temperature and Duration

As with the adult animals, the biological processes taking place inside reptile eggs are determined by the temperature at which they are kept. The warmer the environment is, the quicker the eggs develop; the cooler the environment is, the longer it takes the eggs to complete their development.

This basic principle holds true for softshell turtles. However, this does not mean that their eggs can be incubated at any temperature. Eggs kept below the minimum acceptable temperature will fail to live, just as those kept above the maximum acceptable temperature.

The ideal temperature for softshell turtle egg incubation is about 80 degrees Fahrenheit (26.6 degrees Celsius). Most softshell turtle eggs hatch approximately 60 to 85 days after being deposited. However, individuals develop at slightly different speeds, so the young may hatch over a period of days. In some cases, the first and last hatchling to emerge from the eggs may be separated by a week's time.

Unlike many other turtles, whose sex is determined by the temperature at which they are incubated, the sex of softshell turtles is determined genetically, as it is in snakes, birds and mammals.

Neonatal Husbandry

Observe the hatchlings as they emerge from their shells. Some turtles will remain in their shells for several days while they absorb the rest of their egg yolk. This is perfectly normal, and you should NOT remove such turtles from their eggs. Allow the turtle to absorb the entire yolk and exit the egg on his own.

If for some reason, the egg becomes destroyed (such as through the activities of the clutchmates), move the turtle into a clean, plastic container with about 1/4 inch of water in the bottom. Do not pull the yolk free, and try to keep it from drying out.

Once the turtles have hatched and absorbed their egg yolk, they are ready to move to the nursery. The nursery container should be constructed from a small plastic storage box (you can split the clutch among several different boxes to reduce the stress on the hatchlings).

Add an inch or so of water to the bottom of the cage, and provide them with basking platforms and heat lamps as you would with adults. You can house a few hatchlings together in the same habitat, but avoid overcrowding them, which can lead to squabbles and injuries. Be sure there are more places to bask than there are turtles in the tank.

You can offer food as soon as you like, but many will not begin feeding for a few days.

Chapter 15: Further Reading

Never stop learning more about your new pet's natural history, biology and captive care. This is the only way to ensure that you are providing your new pet with the highest quality of life possible.

It's always more fun to interact with your turtle than read about him, but by accumulating more knowledge, you'll be better able to provide him with a high quality of life.

Books

Bookstores and online book retailers offer a treasure trove of information that will advance your quest for knowledge. While books represent an additional cost involved in reptile care, you can consider it an investment in your pet's well-being. Your local library may also carry some books about leopard geckos, which you can borrow for no charge.

University libraries are a great place for finding old, obscure or academically oriented books about leopard geckos. You may not be allowed to borrow these books if you are not a student, but you can view and read them at the library.

Herpetology: An Introductory Biology of Amphibians and Reptiles
By Laurie J. Vitt, Janalee P. Caldwell
Top of Form
Bottom of Form
Academic Press, 2013

Understanding Reptile Parasites: A Basic Manual for Herpetoculturists & Veterinarians
By Roger Klingenberg D.V.M.
Advanced Vivarium Systems, 1997

Infectious Diseases and Pathology of Reptiles: Color Atlas and Text
Elliott Jacobson
CRC Press

Designer Reptiles and Amphibians
Richard D. Bartlett, Patricia Bartlett
Barron's Educational Series

Turtles of the World
Franck Bonin, Bernard Devaux, Alain Dupré
JHU Press

Turtle Conservation
Michael W. Klemens
Smithsonian Institution Press

Magazines

Because magazines are typically published monthly or bi-monthly, they occasionally offer more up-to-date information than books do. Magazine articles are obviously not as comprehensive as books typically are, but they still have considerable value.

Reptiles Magazine
www.reptilesmagazine.com/
Covering reptiles commonly kept in captivity.

Practical Reptile Keeping
http://www.practicalreptilekeeping.co.uk/
Practical Reptile Keeping is a popular publication aimed at beginning and advanced hobbies. Topics include the care and maintenance of popular reptiles as well as information on wild reptiles.

Websites

The internet has made it much easier to find information about reptiles than it has ever been.

However, you must use discretion when deciding which websites to trust. While knowledgeable breeders, keepers and academics operate some websites, many who maintain reptile-oriented websites lack the same dedication and scientific rigor.

Anyone with a computer and internet connection can launch a website and say virtually anything they want about geckos. Accordingly, as with all other research, consider the source of the information before making any husbandry decisions.

Note: at the time of printing, all the websites below were working. As the internet changes rapidly, some sites might no longer be live when you read this book. That is, of course, out of our control.

The Reptile Report
www.thereptilereport.com/
The Reptile Report is a news-aggregating website that accumulates interesting stories and features about reptiles from around the world.

Kingsnake.com
www.kingsnake.com
After starting as a small website for gray-banded kingsnake enthusiasts, Kingsnake.com has become one of the largest reptile-oriented portals in the hobby. The site features classified advertisements, a breeder directory, message forums and other resources.

The Vivarium and Aquarium News
www.vivariumnews.com/
The online version of the former print publication, The Vivarium and Aquarium News provides in-depth coverage of different reptiles and amphibians in a captive and wild context.

Journals
Journals are the primary place professional scientists turn when they need to learn about turtles. While they may not make light reading, hobbyists stand to learn a great deal from journals.

Herpetologica
www.hljournals.org/
Published by The Herpetologists' League, Herpetologica, and its companion publication, Herpetological Monographs cover all aspects of reptile and amphibian research.

Journal of Herpetology
www.ssarherps.org/
Produced by the Society for the Study of Reptiles and Amphibians, the Journal of Herpetology is a peer-reviewed publication covering a variety of reptile-related topics.

Copeia
www.asihcopeiaonline.org/
Copeia is published by the American Society of Ichthyologists and Herpetologists. A peer-reviewed journal, Copeia covers all aspects of the biology of reptiles, amphibians and fish.

Nature
www.nature.com/
Although Nature covers all aspects of the natural world, many issues contain information that turtle enthusiasts are sure to find interesting.

Supplies

You can obtain most of what you need to maintain leopard gecko through your local pet store, big-box retailer or hardware store, but online retailers offer another option.

Just be sure that you consider the shipping costs for any purchase, to ensure you aren't "saving" yourself a few dollars on the product, yet spending several more dollars to get the product delivered.

Big Apple Pet Supply
http://www.bigappleherp.com
Big Apple Pet Supply carries most common husbandry equipment, including heating devices, water dishes and substrates.

LLLReptile
http://www.lllreptile.com
LLL Reptile carries a wide variety of husbandry tools, heating devices, lighting products and more.

Doctors Foster and Smith
http://www.drsfostersmith.com
Foster and Smith is a veterinarian-owned retailer that supplies husbandry-related items to pet keepers.

Support Organizations

Sometimes, the best way to learn about leopard geckos is to reach out to other keepers and breeders. Check out these organizations, and search for others in your geographic area.

The National Reptile & Amphibian Advisory Council
http://www.nraac.org/
The National Reptile & Amphibian Advisory Council seeks to educate the hobbyists, legislators and the public about reptile and amphibian related issues.

American Veterinary Medical Association
www.avma.org
The AVMA is a good place for Americans to turn if you are having trouble finding a suitable reptile veterinarian.

The World Veterinary Association
http://www.worldvet.org/
The World Veterinary Association is a good resource for finding suitable reptile veterinarians worldwide.

References

Anderson, S. P. (2003). The Phylogenetic Definition of Reptilia. *Systematic Biology.*

Badenhorst D, S. R. (2013). A ZZ/ZW microchromosome system in the spiny softshell turtle, Apalone spinifera, reveals an intriguing sex chromosome conservation in Trionychidae. *Chromosome Research .*

Crawford, N. G. (2012). A phylogenomic analysis of turtles. *Molecular Phylogenetics and Evolution.*

Greenbaum E, C. J. (2001). Sexual differentiation in the spiny softshell turtle (Apalone spinifera), a species with genetic sex determination. *Journal of Experimental Zoology.*

Khalil, F. (1947). Excretion in Reptiles. *Journal of Biological Chemisty.*

Moll, J. L. (1973). Latitudinal Reproductive Variation within a Single Subspecies of Painted Turtle, Chrysemys picta bellii. *Herpetologica.*

Mu Y, Z. B. (2015). Temperature-dependent sex determination ruled out in the Chinese soft-shelled turtle (Pelodiscus sinensis) via molecular cytogenetics and incubation experiments across populations. *Sexual Development.*

PLUMMER, M. V. (2007). NEST EMERGENCE OF SMOOTH SOFTSHELL TURTLE (APALONE MUTICA) HATCHLINGS. *Herpetological Conservation and Biology.*

Roy D. Nagle, M. V. (2003). PARENTAL INVESTMENT, EMBRYO GROWTH, AND HATCHLING LIPID RESERVES IN SOFTSHELL TURTLES (APALONE MUTICA) FROM ARKANSAS. *Herpetologica.*

Index

Achilles tendonitis, 84
bladder, 12
Bleach, 52
Breeding, 54, 67, 68
cage, 26
carapace, 9
circulatory, 11
Costs, 25
digestive system, 11
eggs, 13, 29, 62, 65, 67, 69, 70, 71, 72, 73, 74, 75
eyes, 28, 29
Feeding, 53
Gender, 54
heart, 12
Heat, 39, 40
Heat Cables, 40
Heat Tape, 40
Homemade Cages, 34
husbandry, 78, 80
Husbandry, 76
lungs, 12
Maintenance, 50
Myths, 26
online, 77
parasites, 64
pulmonary, 11
Reproductive, 12
Rheostats, 42
Size, 33
skeletons, 11
skull, 11
Temperature, 37
Thermostats, 42
veterinarian, 52, 80, 81

Published by IMB Publishing 2017

ALL RIGHTS RESERVED. This book contains material protected under International and Federal Copyright Laws and Treaties.

Any unauthorized reprint or use of this material is strictly prohibited. No part of this book may be reproduced or transmitted in any form or by any means, electronic, mechanical or otherwise, including photocopying or recording, or by any information storage and retrieval system without express written permission from the author.

Copyright and Trademarks: This publication is Copyrighted 2017 by IMB Publishing. All products, publications, software and services mentioned and recommended in this publication are protected by trademarks. In such instance, all trademarks & copyright belong to the respective owners. All rights reserved. No part of this book may be reproduced or transferred in any form or by any means, graphic, electronic, or mechanical, including photocopying, recording, taping, or by any information storage retrieval system, without the written permission of the authors. Pictures used in this book are either royalty free pictures bought from stock-photo websites or have the source mentioned underneath the picture.

Disclaimer and Legal Notice: This product is not legal or medical advice and should not be interpreted in that manner. You need to do your own due-diligence to determine if the content of this product is right for you. The author and the affiliates of this product are not liable for any damages or losses associated with the content in this product. While every attempt has been made to verify the information shared in this publication, neither the author nor the affiliates assume any responsibility for errors, omissions or contrary interpretation of the subject matter herein. Any perceived slights to any specific person(s) or organization(s) are purely unintentional. We have no control over the nature, content and availability of the web sites listed in this book. The inclusion of any web site links does not necessarily imply a recommendation or endorse the views expressed within them. IMB Publishing takes no responsibility for, and will not be liable for, the websites being temporarily unavailable or being removed from the Internet. The accuracy and completeness of information provided herein and opinions stated herein are not guaranteed or warranted to produce any particular results, and the advice and strategies, contained herein may not be suitable for every individual. The author shall not be liable for any loss incurred as a consequence of the use and application, directly or indirectly, of any information presented in this work. This publication is designed to provide information in regards to the subject matter covered. The information included in this book has been compiled to give an overview of the subject s and detail some of the symptoms, treatments etc. that are available to people with this condition. It is not intended to give medical advice. For a firm diagnosis of your condition, and for a treatment plan suitable for you, you should consult your doctor or consultant. The writer of this book and the publisher are not responsible for any damages or negative consequences following any of the treatments or methods highlighted in this book. Website links are for informational purposes and should not be seen as a personal endorsement; the same applies to the products detailed in this book. The reader should also be aware that although the web links included were correct at the time of writing, they may become out of date in the future.

www.ingramcontent.com/pod-product-compliance
Lightning Source LLC
Chambersburg PA
CBHW060851050426
42453CB00008B/932